AMERICAN
HERITAGE

February 1962 · Volume XIII, Number 2

War engenders passions, and civil war the bitterest.
In this 1861 northern print by E. B. and E. C. Kellogg,
of Hartford, Connecticut, the Union eagle guards its
nest of states; the Confederate "eggs" have already
hatched out various unsavory creatures, except for
Tennessee, but it too seceded and was labeled "rotten."
You could not remain neutral in that war: Maryland,
where conflicting loyalties divided many a family,
was called a "bad egg," as was "addled" Kentucky,
yet both of them eventually remained in the nest.

AMERICAN HERITAGE

The Magazine of History

PUBLISHER
James Parton

EDITORIAL DIRECTOR
Joseph J. Thorndike, Jr.

SENIOR EDITOR
Bruce Catton

EDITOR
Oliver Jensen

ASSOCIATE EDITORS
Richard M. Ketchum
Joan Paterson Mills
Robert L. Reynolds

ASSISTANT EDITORS
Robert Cowley, Meryle Evans
Stephen W. Sears

CONTRIBUTING EDITOR
Margery Darrell

LIBRARIAN
Caroline Backlund

COPY EDITOR
Beverly Hill

ASSISTANT: Suzanne Adessa

SENIOR ART DIRECTOR
Irwin Glusker

ART DIRECTOR
Murray Belsky

STAFF PHOTOGRAPHER: Herbert Loebel

ADVISORY BOARD
Allan Nevins, *Chairman*

Ray A. Billington   Alvin M. Josephy, Jr.
Carl Carmer   Richard P. McCormick
Albert B. Corey   Harry Shaw Newman
Christopher Crittenden Howard H. Peckham
Marshall B. Davidson   S. K. Stevens
Louis C. Jones   Arthur M. Schlesinger, Sr.

AMERICAN HERITAGE is published every two months by American Heritage Publishing Co., Inc., 551 Fifth Avenue, New York 17, N.Y. Correspondence about subscriptions should be addressed to: American Heritage Subscription Office, 383 West Center Street, Marion, Ohio. Single Copies: $3.95. Annual Subscriptions: $15.00 in U.S. & Canada; $16.00 elsewhere.

An annual Index of AMERICAN HERITAGE is published every February, priced at $1.00. A Cumulative Index of Volumes VI—X is available at $3.00.

AMERICAN HERITAGE will consider but assumes no responsibility for unsolicited material.
Title registered U.S. Patent Office.
Second class postage paid at New York, N.Y.

Sponsored by

American Association for State & Local History · Society of American Historians

CONTENTS   *February 1962 · Volume XIII, Number 2*

COVER: In 1908, near the very end of a long career devoted to painting the American West, Frederic Remington portrayed *The Sentinel,* his weapon at the ready, ears alert for any suspicious sound, standing guard over a train of emigrant wagons. The trials of that long journey across two thousand miles of endless plains, barren deserts, and man-killing mountain trails are recounted by George R. Stewart in "The Prairie Schooner Got Them There," which begins on page 4. The picture is now in the Remington Art Memorial in Ogdensburg, New York. *Back Cover: The Cat,* painted about 1840 by an unknown artist, is from the exhibition—currently on tour—entitled "101 Masterpieces of American Primitive Painting from the Collection of Edgar William and Bernice Chrysler Garbisch."

Samuel Colman's Emigrant Train *shows covered wagons at a shallow ford on the Oregon Trail. Deeper streams were crossed by rais-*

The Prairie Schooner Got

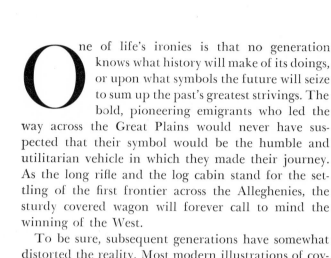

covered wagon stands as the symbol of the winning of the West

ing the wagon beds or by floating them to the opposite shore.

Them There

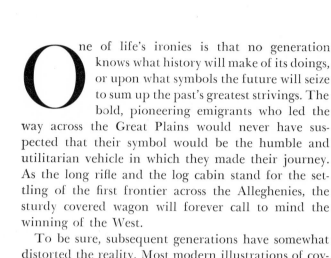

By GEORGE R. STEWART

One of life's ironies is that no generation knows what history will make of its doings, or upon what symbols the future will seize to sum up the past's greatest strivings. The bold, pioneering emigrants who led the way across the Great Plains would never have suspected that their symbol would be the humble and utilitarian vehicle in which they made their journey. As the long rifle and the log cabin stand for the settling of the first frontier across the Alleghenies, the sturdy covered wagon will forever call to mind the winning of the West.

To be sure, subsequent generations have somewhat distorted the reality. Most modern illustrations of covered wagons, for example, depict the huge and lumbering Conestoga, with its boat-shaped bed and sloping sides, its cover overhanging front and rear to give the whole a "swayback" appearance. Originating about 1750 in Pennsylvania, it flourished for a century. But it was almost never used beyond the Missouri except by freighters along the Santa Fe Trail. The Conestoga was uselessly heavy for the long pull to Oregon or California, and most of the few that were ill-advisedly taken on that journey had to be abandoned somewhere along the road. Physically, the emigrants' vehicles were about the same as the so-called "movers' wagons" that had taken earlier travelers on shorter, less heroic journeys. To go from one point to another farther west —from Connecticut to Ohio, say, or from Georgia to Alabama—the mover merely packed his wagon, hitched up, and went off over an already established road. He passed through a familiar type of country. He bought needed supplies at village stores. If a wagon broke down, or an ox died, or a child took sick, he could find whatever assistance was needed. The journey was seldom of more than a few hundred miles, and was not likely to require more than a month or six weeks.

Then, about 1840, the situation changed. Partly the change was geographical; partly political; partly, perhaps, psychological. Geographically, the central frontier now lay in Iowa and Missouri. Beyond it, in what is now eastern Nebraska and Kansas, there was some land that by the standards of the time was potentially good for farming. But this was a rather narrow belt, and in the eyes of a farmer of 1840 there was nothing

Mormon wagons heading for the ferry across the Missouri at Council Bluffs, Iowa, in 1846. This and the painting opposite are the work of William Henry Jackson, pre-eminent photographer of the West, who after his retirement in 1929 at the age of eighty-six was asked by the Oregon Trail Memorial Association to re-create on canvas the adventurous old days. The mealtime sketch below and its mate opposite were made in 1866, a lifetime before, as young Jackson headed west.

BOTH SKETCHES, SCOTTS BLUFF NATIONAL MONUMENT, GERING, NEBRASKA

much to be expected of it. Moreover, there was the political barrier, since Congress had established this nearer region as Indian territory. There was also room for settlers in Minnesota, but this was a cold and inhospitable region from the point of view of a southerner—and the cutting edge of the frontier was largely southern. Finally, by 1840 there had been a good deal of favorable publicity about both Oregon and California. The latter, to be sure, was still a part of Mexico. "But," anyone could say, "look at what happened in Texas!"

Thus the problem in 1840 was vastly different from that faced by earlier movers. The distance to be traversed totaled about two thousand miles, and it must be made in one jump, between winter and winter. The intervening country was unsettled, so that any emergency must be met with the materials at hand. There was nothing that could be called an established road for wagons. The country was not the well-watered and generally benign eastern terrain, but was largely mountainous and arid. The Indians had not already retreated before the advancing white man, but were wholly untamed; many were powerful and warlike.

BOTH PAINTINGS FROM *The Old West Speaks*, BY HOWARD DRIGGS, © 1956 BY PRENTICE-HALL, INC.

Thus presented, the odds seem impossible. A saying later current in California begins, "The cowards never started." One would be inclined to go a little further and say, "Only the madmen started!" Yet start they did, and after some failures they were successful. Thus, rightly, an epic achievement placed the covered wagon in its present niche of glory.

Behind that achievement lay a psychic drive, a desire, almost a passion, to keep moving—and there was only one direction: westward! Many of the emigrants have left records of their motives. Negatively, they specify the wish to escape the agricultural depression that followed the panic of 1837, or the desire to get away from the malaria that raged throughout the Mississippi Valley. Positively, they mention the attractions of Oregon and California—the climate, the rich farmland, the chance to get ahead. Many went out of the sheer love of adventure—and an occasional one, like the absconding banker in the emigration of 1841, because he was fleeing the police.

The other motives seem to have been obscure to the emigrants themselves, but hindsight enables us to see them clearly. With many of these people, moving had

Thousands of emigrants remembered Echo Canyon, Utah, a few miles east of Great Salt Lake, where the trail wound along the foot of towering red sandstone cliffs and beside a welcome stream of fresh water. George Donner took his ill-starred party through here in 1846, the Mormons followed the next year, and eventually the Union Pacific Railroad laid its tracks through the canyon as well. Jackson called the hitching scene below "my first lesson in yoking a wild bull."

7

become a habit, even an ancestral habit. Their journey to the Pacific Coast was not their first one. Joseph Chiles was only thirty-one years old when he headed west in '41, but he had already moved from Kentucky to Missouri. George Donner, captain of the ill-fated party in '46, had been born in North Carolina, but had lived in Kentucky, Indiana, Texas, and Illinois. Many, indeed, were Englishmen, Scotsmen, Irishmen, or Germans, to whom the Mississippi Valley was only a way stop. To all of these people, "going west" was as natural as swimming upstream is to a salmon.

Mere monotony and ennui must have been a second unconscious but important reason. After a man, or a woman, had vegetated on a frontier farm for ten years, sheer boredom would be likely to make the risks of the journey seem rather attractive. One man put it simply. He had always liked to fish, he said, and he had heard that there was good fishing in Oregon.

These, then, were the forces that drove men west. How would they get there?

First among those factors that made desire practical were the trappers and missionaries who had already gained some knowledge of the country. This knowledge, indeed, was far from complete. The idea that the mountain men "knew every foot of the West" is sheer nonsense, as the history of the migration makes startlingly clear. Still, what they did know was invaluable. They had even taken wheeled vehicles—carts, generally—a long way along the road.

The ignorance of the first emigrants and the comparative knowledge of these others is strikingly demonstrated by the situation in '41. The emigrants had assembled their wagons on the Missouri frontier, ready to start, when they discovered that not one of them had the slightest idea of what the route was. Luckily, they were able to attach themselves to a company of

8

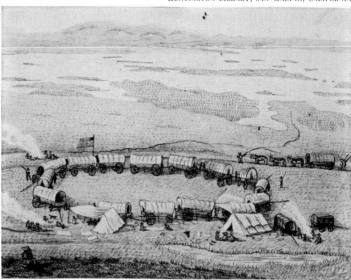

Stopping for the night *along the trail was a happy time (unless the weather was bad): it offered relief for cramped muscles and aching bones as well as an opportunity for talk and laughter while the aroma of cooking filled the air. Here are three different views of it: a sketch (above) made by J. Goldsborough Bruff, who joined the rush for California gold; a painting (left) by Benjamin Franklin Reinhart; and a photograph (below) taken by an unknown hand on an unknown date. Bruff's sketch was made along the Platte River, thirty miles above Ash Hollow, Nebraska, in 1849; wagons did indeed park in a circle, for it offered such good protection that Indians almost never attacked, preferring to wait until the wagons were strung out along the trail (see page 14). Reinhart's romanticized painting contains several inaccuracies: the wagons are of the cumbersome Conestoga type, for example; though the Conestoga had a proud history in early America, it was too heavy and too awkward for the cross-country journey. The photograph is far closer to reality. In all probability, the men of the party are watering the stock in the grove of trees at left.*

To pull their wagons, emigrants and freight operators used both oxen (above) and mules (below and opposite), and each beast had its champions. Price ordinarily determined the choice: an ox could be bought for one third the cost of a mule, and in the end most people who headed west were "ox-team emigrants." The photograph below was taken in 1866 in Denver, on what is now Market Street, between Fifteenth and Sixteenth streets. Frontier towns in those days grew quickly, supplying the wagon trains passing through and, afterward, those emigrants who chose to settle down instead of pushing on; among the visible stores are a land office, a hardware and saddle shop, and a leather warehouse. The trail through the Rockies was hazardous, as the photograph on the opposite page, also taken in Colorado, shows. This string of empty freight wagons, evidently heading back east for a new load of goods, threads its way along a prepared road, rather than a primitive trail. Even so, a sudden hard rain could turn such a road to gumbo, and a rock slide could obliterate entire sections of it, causing interminable delays. Those fortunate enough to escape hazards such as these faced other perils, some of which are described in detail on the following pages.

missionaries led by the famous Belgian Jesuit Pierre Jean De Smet and guided by "Broken Hand" Fitzpatrick, one of the famous mountain men. This guidance served the emigrants excellently for about half the distance, and then they were forced to press on into a country about which even the mountain men could tell them little—and with disastrous results. Still, however limited, the information and leadership supplied by the mountain men—Fitzpatrick, Joseph Walker, Caleb Greenwood, Isaac Hitchcock—were essential aids to the migration.

Granted the desire and some information, the frontier people next had to make the choice among three traditional modes of transportation: the cart, the pack train, or the wagon.

The two-wheeled cart seems scarcely to have been considered. At first glance, this seems curious. Carts were in use on many farms. They were strong and highly maneuverable. To the south, in Mexico, the *carreta* had served excellently during the magnificent push of the frontier northward. To the north, the so-called Red River cart, pulled by two or three mules in tandem, had become the standard means of transport on the Canadian prairies; American fur traders had adopted them, too, and had taken long trains of them as far as the Rocky Mountains.

But the cart was primarily adapted to the transportation of goods, not of families. And the emigration was primarily a family matter. A house on wheels was what was needed, and this the cart simply did not provide. Occasionally, when his team was reduced by death or exhaustion, some emigrant cut his wagon down to cart-size and thus was able to continue, but this is about all we hear of carts in the migration proper.

On the other hand, the pack train had its definite place. The mule, and less commonly the horse, already served as a pack animal for the mountain men, and during the migration, notably in 1849, was often employed. The advantages were obvious. The greater speed of movement meant carrying a smaller weight of supplies; the over-all time could be cut by at least a month, and the dangerous stretches of desert could be traversed more quickly. Pack trains could ford streams and cross mountains and rough country much more easily than could wagons.

But for migrating families the disadvantages of the pack train were extreme. Most farm women could ride, but few could withstand the day-after-day jouncing that would add up to two thousand miles. If the wife was pregnant (and many set out in that condition), it was obviously foolish to attempt such a ride. Small children were equally unsuited to the pack train. And there were other handicaps. As an ox driver noted: "The pack-mule companies are a pitiful set of slaves.

They have to sit on their mules roasting in the sun all day. If they get down to walk or rest themselves, they must be bothered leading the animals. When they stop at night, they must unpack everything. In the mornings they have to repack everything."

Finally, in the event of accident or severe illness to one of its members, the pack train faced disaster. In a wagon train a man with a broken leg or a case of dysentery could be trundled along. If such a situation arose in a pack train (and difficulties were only to be expected), there was no humane solution. The barbarous abandonment of comrades on the road, such as was recorded in '49 especially, must have resulted from this dilemma.

Pack-train companies, therefore, generally consisted of young men, willing to risk their chances of getting through quickly against their chances of not getting through at all.

There remained, then, the wagon. Its disadvantages were obvious—it was slow, heavy, cumbersome, subject to breakage, difficult to take across rivers, ravines, and mountains or through rocky country. But it served as a moving home, involved less daily unpacking and repacking, allowed more pounds to be transported per animal, supplied an ambulance for the sick, and—when properly placed in formation—offered a fortress against attack. Thus it became a standard vehicle of the westward migration.

The wagon consisted of three parts—body, top, and running gear. The body, or bed, was a wooden box—often, indeed, so-called—nine or ten feet long and about four feet wide. Generally the sides and ends, about two feet high, went up perpendicularly, but on wagons of the so-called Murphy type they flared outward, as if imitating the Conestoga in miniature. Many emigrants built a false floor twelve or fifteen inches from the bottom of the bed. The lower space was divided into compartments and used for storing reserve supplies. With this clutter out of the way, the false floor was used for ordinary living.

The wagon boxes served their purpose, were subjected to no particular strain, and gave no trouble. They are seldom mentioned at all in the diaries. The top or cover was the most conspicuous part of the whole outfit, and has supplied the distinguishing adjective in the phrase "covered wagon."

This top was of canvas (then usually called twill) or else of some cloth which had been waterproofed with paint or linseed oil. It was supported by bows of bent hickory, usually five or six in number. On the ordinary straight-sided bed these went straight up. There was thus no overhang at front or rear and no

A prairie fire, like the one opposite painted by William Ranney in 1848, was among the most terrifying experiences on the trail. A traveler of that period who had survived one never forgot it. "How awful, and how grand!" he wrote. "The wind, new changed and freshened, to the right and rear, was tossing the flames towards us . . . We were speedily under way, with as much earnestness of advance as that of righteous Lot, in his escape from burning Sodom." If a party's stock stampeded, they were in desperate straits indeed. The Bruff sketch at right above depicts another kind of danger; this accident took place in 1849, forty miles above St. Joseph, Missouri. The wagon in the undated photo below had to be abandoned after it bogged down in quicksand.

"There are no friendly Indians on the Plains."
In these words an emigrant of 1869 named the fear that was a silent passenger in every covered wagon entering upon the vast emptiness west of the Mississippi during the bitter Indian battles after the Civil War. The savages were fighting for their homeland, and in this they had an immeasurable advantage over the emigrants: they knew the country in great detail, and the white men did not. The savages could, therefore, easily post spies upon high ground— as in The Ambush *(right), painted in 1883 by the Frenchman Paul Frenzeny, who had toured the West for* Harper's Weekly *in 1873-74. Having chosen the most advantageous time and place, the hidden foe could then launch an attack, as visualized by the German-born artist Charles Wimar, who in 1854 painted the romantic scene above. It represents a gold-rush caravan besieged by hostile Indians—actually a relatively rare incident in the prewar years.*

swayback. Flaps at the front and a "puckering string" at the back allowed ventilation or complete closing. Inside, the wagon was thus a tiny room, about ten by four, with sides partly of wood and partly of canvas rising almost perpendicularly to a height of four or five feet and then arching over. A man could stand upright along the center line. On wagons with flaring sides the bows followed the lines of the sides before arching over, producing a more cylindrical effect, with perhaps a front and rear overhang.

The top effectively protected goods and people against the weather. In an upset, it might be torn and some of the bows broken, and in thick forest country overhanging branches sometimes ripped the cloth, but there was not much country of that kind. When going head-on into the strong westerly winds of the plains, some companies put the tops down to reduce wind resistance. But on the whole the tops, like the boxes, produced few problems.

Not so the running gear. In the numerous booklets of advice surviving from the period, there is always the admonition that the wagons should be light and strong. Obviously the two qualities are somewhat incompatible, and even the best materials and workmanship

The goal of most emigrants was the rich Pacific slope, and the painting above, entitled The Promised Land, shows one family that made it. Captain Andrew Jackson Grayson—who was to become "the Audubon of the Pacific"—and his wife and son posed for the California artist W. S. Jewett in 1850.

could not always produce a vehicle that would get through without breakage.

By the mid-nineteenth century the construction of running gear had reached a high degree of sophistication. Readers of Oliver Wendell Holmes' poem about the one-hoss shay will remember the care and the many different woods that went into construction of the deacon's masterpiece. Though the emigrant's wagon might not have been that carefully constructed, it could well have had hubs of elm or Osage orange, spokes of oak, felloes of ash, and tongue and hounds of hickory. Moreover, the tires were of iron, and iron was used for reinforcement at critical points.

Yet lightness was essential too, or the teams would be worn out by the mere dead weight of the wagon. The result, as in the airplane decades later, was a compromise. In the end, breakages were frequent, precipitating many a crisis and many a tragedy.

Tongues snapped on sharp turns. Front axles gave way on sudden down-drops. These were the commonest accidents, and were taken almost as routine. "Occasionally we break a tongue or an axletree," wrote an emigrant of '49, as if thinking it all in the day's work. Some emigrants carried extra parts, but this added to the total weight, and so was doubtful practice. Usually the nearest suitable tree supplied timber, though "nearest" was sometimes not very near. In '46, when one of J. F. Reed's wagons suffered a broken axle near Great Salt Lake, his teamsters had to go fifteen miles to find a tree large enough to furnish a replacement. Not many were as unlucky as Ira Butterfield, who in 1861 snapped both axles at once while crossing Skull Creek. Fortunately he was with a large, well-equipped company, so that the accident meant only a twenty-four hour delay, and not disaster.

Wheels, however, were irreplaceable; if one broke, the wagon might have to be abandoned. But usually, wheels were extremely tough and rarely gave way except in the roughest mountain passages. True, many a

CONTINUED ON PAGE 98

The casualties: Emigrants without number perished by the wayside—of cholera, hunting mishaps, childbed fever, Indian raids—so that the way west was marked by graves (right). The site of these is unknown, but it may be near Humboldt Sink, Nevada, one of the worst stretches of the whole route.

The flag goes up at Camp McCalla, Guantanamo Bay, in a photograph widely distributed by government agencies. In one of the versions, the flag-raiser is a Marine Lieutenant Draper; in another caption, he is a Lieutenant Jenkins, U.S.N. (Several contemporary newspapers democratically make him a Color Sergeant Silvey.) The date given is, variously, June 10, 11, or 12, 1898. Such, sometimes, is history, filled with drama, confusing but generous, with laurels for all.

How We Got
GUANTANAMO

The Cuban situation was confused, but the Marines were ready.
They landed, and our first overseas base was soon well in hand

By COLONEL ROBERT D. HEINL, JR., U.S.M.C.

By May 28, 1898, the uncertainty was over. Admiral Cervera's fleet had been run to ground in the cliff-ringed harbor of Santiago de Cuba. "There can be no doubt," cabled Admiral William T. Sampson to the Navy Department, "of presence of Spanish squadron at Santiago."

After weeks of war nerves, punctuated by rumors of Spanish cruisers off every port on the Atlantic coast and by much backing and filling off Cuba, Commodore Winfield Scott Schley's Flying Squadron had finally spotted the enemy ships at Santiago. The blockade of the Spanish fleet had begun. By urgent cable to the American consul at Kingston, and thence by fast steamer to the coast of Cuba, Secretary of the Navy John D. Long sent Schley his orders: "Unless it is unsafe for your squadron, Department wishes you to remain off Santiago"; then another phrase, whose consequences would bear heavily on American foreign policy six decades later—"*Can not you take possession of Guantanamo, occupy as a coaling station?*"

Secretary Long was not the first to visualize Guantanamo Bay as a potential advance base. It offered a sheltered anchorage covering some fifteen square miles of water. One hundred and fifty-seven years before, while his country was at war with Spain, British Admiral Edward Vernon dropped anchor with sixty-one sail on July 13, 1741, in Walthenham Bay, as the place was then known. Vernon renamed it Cumberland Harbor and occupied it as a base of operations against "St. Jago de Cuba," forty miles westward. Aboard one of Vernon's ships was the novelist Tobias Smollett, later to record the landings at Walthenham Bay in *The Adventures of Roderick Random;* an officer in Vernon's regiment of American marines was Lawrence Washington, half-brother of George, who would give the Admiral's name to his estate beside the Potomac River.

Still earlier, this "large and secure haven," as Guantanamo was described in 1779, had been the lair of pirates plying the Windward Passage. And Columbus, who anchored in the bay on his second voyage, in April, 1494, was so struck with its expanse that he entitled it Puerto Grande.

Protected by dust-brown, scrub-covered mountains against observation or bombardment by sea, and sheltered from the force of hurricanes, Guantanamo Bay was indeed a prize. Moreover, despite its strategic position and a French cable station which linked Cuba with Haiti and thence Europe, the Spanish defenses of Guantanamo in 1898 were unimpressive. True, a brigade of some 7,000 men under General Felix Pareja held the town of Guantanamo, fourteen miles inland from the bay. But in 1898, as it would be again for Fidel Castro, Oriente Province was a cradle of revolution, and General Pareja was hard-pressed to hold his base and the weed-grown railroad that connected it with Caimanera, the fever-ridden, dirty sugar port near the head of the inner bay. All he could spare to defend Guantanamo Bay were the gunboat *Sandoval,* a handful of mines, and a few hundred soldiers occupying the region of Playa del Este (Windward Point) and a fort on Cayo del Toro, guarding the channel which joins the inner to the outer bay. "I continue serving out half rations of everything," Pareja gloomily reported in early June, 1898, "and in that way I expect to reach only the end of the month, above all in bread, as I have no flour of any kind, as I said, and no way of getting any . . ."

Exactly six weeks before the thought of occupying Guantanamo Bay had entered the minds of Secretary Long and his Naval War Board—in fact five days before war was even declared on Spain—the Navy Department had ordered the Marine Corps to organize a battalion for service in Cuba. This battalion, to be composed of "young, strong, and healthy men," was to include five rifle companies (each with its own drummer and fifer) and an artillery company armed with three-inch rapid-fire guns and the latest thing in automatic weapons—the 1895 Colt machine gun, called by the troops, because of its peculiar downward recoil, "Colt's potato-digger."

To command the battalion, whose twenty-four officers and 623 enlisted men included more than one fifth of the entire Corps, Marine headquarters had chosen Lieutenant Colonel Robert W. Huntington, one of the toughest and most demanding officers in the Corps, whose career dated back to the first Bull Run. In the 1870's, finding even the life of a Marine insufficiently challenging, he had sought assignment with the cavalry in order to fight Indians on the frontier. Junior officers and enlisted men still remembered the merciless field problems Huntington set as a major, when he pushed skirmishers back and forth all day through terrain alive with chiggers and infested with poison oak.

Sergeant John Quick won the Medal of Honor for signaling a vital message under fire.

With somewhat greater foresight than the Army, Navy planners had early realized that getting troops to Cuba to fight the Spaniards would require transports. Consequently, while Huntington's men were arriving at the Marine barracks in Brooklyn from posts throughout the East, the Navy Yard was working double shifts to convert the S.S. *Venezuela*, a dingy merchantman, into a suitable expeditionary vessel. Command of this ship, renamed the U.S.S. *Panther*, was entrusted to another Civil War veteran, Commander G. C. Reiter.

At length all was ready. The Spanish minister had been handed his passports on April 20; two days later, Huntington's battalion paraded behind a band through Brooklyn's cheering crowds and embarked on the *Panther*, the first American troops to leave for the war. In her holds was a carefully selected assortment of campaign equipment, reported by the quartermaster to include: ". . . mosquito netting, woolen and linen clothing, heavy and light weight underwear, three months' supply of provisions, wheelbarrows, push carts, pickaxes, shovels, barbed-wire cutters, wall and shelter tents, and a full supply of medical stores . . ." Whereas Army troops, slowly mobilizing for Cuba, were issued long Krags and black-powder Springfields, the rifle the Marines carried was the Navy's Lee. It was a thoroughly modern weapon which used smokeless powder; if its caliber, 6 mm. or .236 inches, was dainty, its velocity was high. "Campaign suits of brown linen"—the very first in the armed forces—were the Marines' uniform ("comfortable, businesslike," announced the quartermaster), while "felt campaign hats," these an Army innovation, were on order.

But Cuba was not the first stop: all through May the Marines lay in Key West, sweating aboard ship for four weeks, then taking field training ashore under Huntington's eye. Reports told them of Dewey's victory at Manila; of the gallant action off Cienfuegos, when Navy launches grappled and cut some of the cables under fire from Spanish batteries; of the U.S.S. *St. Louis*'s failure to cut Guantanamo's cables on May 19; of the *Oregon*'s dash from the Pacific around the Horn to join the war. And still the Marines stayed at Key West, and still they trained.

"Excellent Sir," began General Pareja's letter to his commander at Santiago:

The 7th day at dawn brought seven ships before the port of Caimanera. They fired grapeshot and all kinds of projectiles on the Playa del Este and Cayo Toro until they set fire to the fort on Playa del Este, and burning the house of the pilots . . . The American squadron in possession of the outer bay has taken it as if for a harbor of rest, they being anchored as if in one of their own ports . . .

Although the unhappy General's count of ships was inaccurate (there were but three, the U.S.S. *Marblehead* and the *Yankee*, and the auxiliary cruiser *St. Louis*), the U.S. Navy had indeed arrived at Guantanamo Bay on June 7, chasing the Spanish gunboat *Sandoval*, which had only seven rounds of ammunition left, to shelter behind the mine fields in the upper bay. The commander of the naval force was the captain of the *Marblehead*, Bowman H. McCalla, a stern, walrus-mustached "sundowner" * of the old Navy and central figure in the "Old Blood-Tub" courts-martial which had followed the desertion of a third of his crew during a single cruise in 1889.

As soon as McCalla's ships were seen to have disposed of the forts and the unfortunate *Sandoval*, two Cuban guerrilla officers made their way out to the *Marblehead* to announce that they held the western side of the bay. These officers brought word from General Calixto Garcia, of "A Message to Garcia" fame, that his forces were at the disposal of the Americans, and prayed for them to land.

On the same day that Commander McCalla anchored in Guantanamo Bay "as if for a harbor of rest," the Marines at Key West received telegraphic orders to break camp and re-embark. Late at night two days later, on June 9, the *Panther* hove to off Santiago, where it received Admiral Sampson's orders to proceed to Guantanamo Bay and land Marines immediately. To screen the landing and protect the proposed position on Fisherman's Point, a group of forty Marines from the battleship *Oregon* and twenty from McCal-

* He earned this epithet because he was so strict that he would require all midshipmen to return aboard from liberty at sundown, just when, of course, a young officer's life grows interesting.

la's *Marblehead,* commanded by Captain M. C. Goodrell, would act as a covering force while Huntington disembarked his battalion from the *Panther.* Early on the bright morning of June 10, these sixty Marines landed on a bit of beach, Playa del Este, just south of Fisherman's Point, which defines the eastern side of the entrance to Guantanamo Bay. A bluejacket diarist, Seaman Cross of the *Oregon,* captured the moment:

June 10. we went down to Guantanamo Bay to put some coal on and landed Marines in the Morning. we wer the first to put foot on Cuban soil in this war. The 9th the Marblehead and Dolphin Bombarded the place and made them look like Munkys; they ran away and left every thing behind them.

That afternoon under the guns of the *Oregon,* the *Marblehead,* and the monitor *Yosemite* (like many officers present, also a Civil War veteran), Huntington's Marine battalion landed in cutters towed by the steam launches from the ships. Tents were put up on what appeared to be the most appropriate site: the slopes of the hill overlooking the bay, atop which Pareja's blockhouse had stood. As a supposed precaution against yellow fever, the Marines set fire to a handful of adjacent shacks. All the while ships' bands played ragtime, and sweating Marines unloaded the gear and manhandled it ashore. The first United States troops to invade Cuba were on the beach in good order. Not a shot had been fired. "There was an enthusiastic demonstration," said a contemporary account, "as the Stars and Stripes were raised over the first American camp on Cuban soil." To record the event, the Marines even had a combat correspondent, none other than Stephen Crane, author of *The Red Badge of Courage,* now representing the New York *Herald.* Despite the realism of his famous war novel, Crane had yet to receive his baptism of fire.

Save for the usual starts and alarms of a first night ashore, the battalion was unmolested, and next day continued work on the camp. Progress was excellent, according to Seaman Cross: "they expect to have the cable work soon and the Harbor well under Hand . . . the latest report is that the Cubans are flocking in to Huntington's camp."

True enough, Colonel Huntington's first visitor that afternoon was a guerrilla leader, Laborde, styling himself colonel in the Army of Cuba. Laborde, who had helped McCalla with pilotage, brought news of the Spaniards. Several hundred, he reported, were concentrated at Cuzco Hill, near which was a well, the only one in the region, some two miles southeast of the Marine camp.

Laborde might have saved his breath. While he and Huntington were conferring, the Spaniards announced themselves. In a swift ambush, they poured a volley at

close range into a two-man outpost in the thickets, killing both sentinels, whose bodies bore more than eight wounds. Two Marine privates, William Dumphy and Charles McColgan, thereby became the first American soldiers to die in Cuba. The attackers melted away, and all the pursuing patrols found were tracks and spent cartridge cases from the Spaniards' Mausers.

Soon after sundown, snipers fired into the camp, where the Marines lay on their arms. Four times thereafter, each time from a different direction, the enemy Mausers cracked, while the Marines replied with their Lees. "It needs little practice," noted Stephen Crane in his detached way, "to tell the difference in sound between the Lee and the Mauser. The Lee says 'Prut!' . . . The Mauser says 'Pop!'—plainly and frankly pop, like a soda-water bottle being opened close to the ear . . ."

After midnight the Spaniards formed for a night attack. Firing intensified from the ridges and ravines to the south and southeast. Manning battle stations, Marines answered with all their weapons, while the five-inch rapid-fire guns of the *Marblehead* hammered the mountain ridge a half-mile behind the camp. Roused by the din, Crane hugged the ground with ". . . a thousand rifles rattling; with the field guns booming in your ears; with the diabolic Colt automatic clacking; with the roar of the *Marblehead* coming from the bay, and, last, with Mauser bullets sneering always in the air a few inches over one's head."

Whatever their original intentions, the Spaniards found this burst of fire enough to dissuade them from

CONTINUED ON PAGE 94

U.S. MARINE CORPS MUSEUM

Lieutenant Colonel Robert W. Huntington, a veteran of the First Battle of Bull Run, commanded the Marine battalion.

21

Packed like animals in the holds of slave ships, Negroes bound for America were prey to disease, brutal masters, and their own suicidal melancholy. Such was the fearful

MIDDLE PASSAGE

By MALCOLM COWLEY *and* DANIEL P. MANNIX

Long before Europeans appeared on the African coast, the merchants of Timbuktu were exporting slaves to the Moorish kingdoms north of the Sahara. Even the transatlantic slave trade had a long history. There were Negroes in Santo Domingo as early as 1503, and the first twenty slaves were sold in Jamestown, Virginia, about the last week of August, 1619, only twelve years after the colony was founded. But the flush days of the trade were in the eighteenth century, when vast supplies of labor were needed for the sugar plantations in the West Indies and the tobacco and rice plantations on the mainland. From 1700 to 1807, when the trade was legally abolished by Great Britain and the United States, more than seventy thousand Negroes were carried across the Atlantic in any normal year. The trade was interrupted by wars, notably by the American Revolution, but the total New World importation for the century may have amounted to five million enslaved persons.

Most of the slaves were carried on shipboard at some point along the four thousand miles of West African coastline that extend in a dog's leg from the Sahara on the north to the southern desert. Known as the Guinea Coast, it was feared by eighteenth-century mariners, who died there by hundreds and thousands every year.

Contrary to popular opinion, very few of the slaves—possibly one or two out of a hundred—were free Africans kidnapped by Europeans. The slaving captains had, as a rule, no moral prejudice against man-stealing, but they usually refrained from it on the ground of its being a dangerous business practice. A vessel suspected of man-stealing might be "cut off" by the natives, its crew killed, and its cargo of slaves offered for sale to other vessels.

The vast majority of the Negroes brought to America had been enslaved and sold to the whites by other Africans. There were coastal tribes and states, like the Efik kingdom of Calabar, that based their whole economy on the slave trade. The slaves might be prisoners of war, they might have been kidnapped by gangs of black marauders, or they might have been sold with their whole families for such high crimes as adultery, impiety, or, as in one instance, stealing a tobacco pipe. Intertribal wars, the principal source of slaves, were in many cases no more than large-scale kidnapping expeditions. Often they were fomented by Europeans, who supplied both sides with muskets and gunpowder—so many muskets or so much powder for each slave that they promised to deliver on shipboard.

The ships were English, French, Dutch, Danish, Portuguese, or American. Lon-

In a 17th century French engraving, a white slave-buyer looks over shackled blacks.

don, Bristol, and finally Liverpool were the great English slaving ports. By 1790 Liverpool had engrossed five eighths of the English trade and three sevenths of the slave trade of all Europe. Its French rival, Nantes, would soon be ruined by the Napoleonic wars. During the last years of legal slaving, Liverpool's only serious competitors were the Yankee captains of Newport and Bristol, Rhode Island.

Profits from a slaving voyage, which averaged nine or ten months, were reckoned at thirty per cent, after deducting sales commissions, insurance premiums, and all other expenses. The Liverpool merchants became so rich from the slave trade that they invested heavily in mills, factories, mines, canals, and railways. That process was repeated in New England, and the slave trade provided much of the capital that was needed for the industrial revolution.

A slaving voyage was triangular. English textiles, notions, cutlery, and firearms were carried to the Guinea Coast, where they were exchanged for slaves. These were sold in America or the West Indies, and part of the proceeds was invested in colonial products, notably sugar and rice, which were carried back to England on the third leg of the voyage. If the vessel sailed from a New England port, its usual cargo was casks of rum from a Massachusetts distillery. The rum was exchanged in Africa for slaves—often at the rate of two hundred gallons per man—and the slaves were exchanged in the West Indies for molasses, which was carried back to New England to be distilled into rum. A slave ship or Guineaman was expected to show a profit for each leg of its triangular course. But the base of the triangle, the so-called Middle Passage from Africa to the New World with a black cargo, was the most profitable part of the voyage, at the highest cost in human suffering. Let us see what happened in the passage during the flush days of the slave trade.

In the drawing above, made in 1837, Guinea Coast slave-dealers paddle captives to a Portuguese brig. Below, a slave is branded before embarkation.

As soon as an assortment of naked slaves was carried aboard a Guineaman, the men were shackled two by two, the right wrist and ankle of one to the left wrist and ankle of another; then they were sent below. The women—usually regarded as fair prey for the sailors—were allowed to wander by day almost anywhere on the vessel, though they spent the night between decks, in a space partitioned off from that of the men. All the slaves were forced to sleep without covering on bare wooden floors, which were often constructed of unplaned boards. In a stormy passage the skin over their elbows might be worn away to the bare bones.

William Bosman says, writing in 1701, "You would really wonder to see how these slaves live on board; for though their number sometimes amounts to six or seven hundred, yet by the careful management of our masters of ships"—the Dutch masters, in this case—"they are so regulated that it seems incredible: And in this particular our nation exceeds all other Europeans; for as the French, Portuguese and English slave-ships, are always foul and stinking; on the contrary ours are for the most part clean and neat."

Slavers of every nation insisted that their own vessels were the best in the trade. Thus, James Barbot, Jr., who sailed on an English ship to the Congo in 1700, was highly critical of the Portuguese. He admits that they made a great point of baptizing the slaves before taking them on board, but then, "It is pitiful," he says, "to see how they crowd those poor wretches, six hundred and fifty or seven hundred in a ship, the men standing in the hold ty'd to stakes, the women between decks and those that are with child in the great cabin and the children in the steeridge which in that hot climate occasions an intolerable stench." Barbot adds, however, that the Portuguese provided the slaves with coarse thick mats, which were "softer for the poor wretches to lie upon than the bare decks . . . and it would be prudent to imitate the Portuguese in this point." The English, however, did not display that sort of prudence.

There were two schools of thought among the English slaving captains, the "loose-packers" and the "tight-packers." The former argued that by giving the slaves a little more room, better food, and a certain amount of liberty, they reduced the death rate and received a better price for each slave in the West Indies. The tight-packers answered that although the loss of life might be greater on each of their voyages, so too were the net receipts from a larger cargo. If many of the survivors were weak and emaciated, as was often the case, they could be fattened up in a West Indian slave yard before being offered for sale.

The argument between the two schools continued as long as the trade itself, but for many years after 1750 the tight-packers were in the ascendant. So great was the profit on each slave landed alive that hardly a captain refrained from loading his vessel to its utmost capacity. Says the Reverend John Newton, who was a slaving captain before he became a clergyman:

The cargo of a vessel of a hundred tons or a little more is calculated to purchase from 220 to 250 slaves. Their lodging rooms below the deck which are three (for the men, the boys, and the women) besides a place for the sick, are sometimes more than five feet high and sometimes less; and this height is divided toward the middle for the slaves to lie in two rows, one above the other, on each side of the ship, close to each other like books upon a shelf. I have known them so close that the shelf would not easily contain one more.

The poor creatures, thus cramped, are likewise in irons for the most part which makes it difficult for them to turn or move or attempt to rise or to lie down without hurting themselves or each other. Every morning, perhaps, more instances than one are found of the living and the dead fastened together.

Newton was writing in 1788, shortly before a famous parliamentary investigation of the slave trade that lasted four years. One among hundreds of witnesses was Dr. Alexander Falconbridge, who had made four slaving voyages as a surgeon. Falconbridge testified that "he made the most of the room," in stowing the slaves, "and wedged them in. They had not so much room as a man in his coffin either in length or breadth. When he had to enter the slave deck, he took off his shoes to avoid crushing the slaves as he was forced to crawl over them." Falconbridge "had the marks on his feet where the slaves bit and pinched him."

Captain Parrey of the Royal Navy was sent to measure the slave ships at Liverpool and make a report to the House of Commons. That was also in 1788. Parrey discovered that the captains of many slavers possessed a chart showing the dimensions of the half deck, lower deck, hold, platforms, gunroom, orlop, and great cabin, in fact of every crevice into which slaves might be wedged. Miniature black figures were drawn on some of the charts to illustrate the most effective method of packing in the cargo.

On the *Brookes*, which Parrey considered to be typical, every man was allowed a space six feet long by sixteen inches wide (and usually about two feet seven inches high); every woman, a space five feet ten inches long by sixteen inches wide; every boy, five feet by fourteen inches; every girl, four feet six inches by twelve inches. The *Brookes* was a vessel of 320 tons. By a new law passed in 1788 it was permitted to carry 454 slaves, and the chart, which later became famous, showed where 451 of them could be stowed away. Parrey failed to see how the captain could find room for three more. Nevertheless, Parliament was told by reliable witnesses, including Dr. Thomas Trotter, formerly surgeon of the *Brookes*, that before the new law she had carried 600 slaves on one voyage and 609 on another.

The Voyage of the Sable Venus from Angola to the West Indies *was the title of this picture by a British artist, Thomas Stothard, who attempted to apply the allegorical conventions of the Enlightenment to the unpleasant realities of the African slave trade.*

aking on slaves was a process that might be completed in a month or two by vessels trading in Lower Guinea, east and south of the Niger delta. In Upper Guinea, west and north of the delta, the process was longer. It might last from six months to a year or more on the Gold Coast, which supplied the slaves most in demand by the English colonies. Meanwhile the captain was buying Negroes, sometimes one or two a day, sometimes a hundred or more in a single lot, while haggling over each purchase.

Those months when a slaver lay at anchor off the malarial coastline were the most dangerous part of her voyage. Not only was her crew exposed to African fevers and the revenge of angry natives; not only was there the chance of her being taken by pirates or by a hostile man-of-war; but there was also the constant threat of a slave mutiny. Captain Thomas Phillips says, in his account of a voyage made in 1693–94:

When our slaves are aboard we shackle the men two and two, while we lie in port, and in sight of their own country, for 'tis then they attempt to make their escape, and mutiny; to prevent which we always keep centinels upon the hatchways, and have a chest full of small arms, ready loaden and prim'd, constantly lying at hand upon the quarter-deck, together with some granada shells; and two of our quarter-deck guns, pointing on the deck thence, and two more out of the steerage, the door of which is always kept shut, and well barr'd; they are fed twice a day, at 10 in the morning, and 4 in the evening, which is the time they are aptest to mutiny, being all upon the deck; therefore all that time, what of our men are not employ'd in distributing their victuals to them, and settling them, stand to their arms; and some with lighted matches at the great guns that yaun upon them, loaden with partridge, till they have done and gone down to their kennels between decks.

In spite of such precautions, mutinies were frequent on the Coast, and some of them were successful. Even a mutiny that failed might lead to heavy losses among the slaves and the sailors. Thus, we read in the Newport, Rhode Island, *Mercury* of November 18, 1765:

By letters from Capt. Hopkins in a Brig belonging to Providence arrived here from Antigua from the Coast of Africa we learn That soon after he left the Coast, the number of his Men being reduced by Sickness, he was obliged to permit some of the Slaves to come upon Deck to assist the People: These Slaves contrived to release the others, and the whole rose upon the People, and endeavoured to get Possession of the Vessel; but was happily prevented by the Captain and his Men, who killed, wounded and forced overboard, Eighty of them, which obliged the rest to submit.

There are scores of similar items in the colonial newspapers.

William Richardson, a young sailor who shipped on an English Guineaman in 1790, tells of going to the help of a French vessel on which the slaves had risen while it was at anchor. The English seamen jumped into the boats and pulled hard for the Frenchman, but by the time they reached it there were "a hundred slaves in possession of the deck and others tumbling up from below." The slaves put up a desperate resistance. "I could not but admire," Richardson says, "the courage of a fine young black who, though his partner in irons lay dead at his feet, would not surrender but fought with his billet of wood until a ball finished his existence. The others fought as well as they could but what could they do against fire-arms?"

There are fairly detailed accounts of fifty-five mutinies on slavers from 1699 to 1845, not to mention passing references to more than a hundred others. The list of ships "cut off" by the natives—often in revenge for the kidnapping of free Africans—is almost as long. On the record it does not seem that Africans submitted tamely to being carried across the Atlantic like chained beasts. Edward

CONTINUED ON PAGE 103

Above, human cargo huddles on the deck of a slave ship. A rebellious slave hung alive by his ribs to a gallows, below, was depicted by the English poet-engraver William Blake.

25

*For a brief moment in the 1890's,
artistic posters became a cultural
rage—almost a mania—in America*

THE POSTER CRAZE

By EDGAR BREITENBACH

"Is there anything under the sun which people will not collect?" the famous French novelist Balzac once asked. "They collect buttons, walking sticks, fans, political pamphlets and newspapers. One day," he added contemptuously, "they may even collect posters."

And so, inevitably, it came to pass. By 1890, forty years after Balzac's death, poster designing was very much an art, and poster collecting a mania. In Paris, where the fad originated, spirited, gaily colored posters could be seen all over the city, advertising everything from art exhibits and little magazines to the lighthearted pleasures of the music hall. Products of *art nouveau*—that widespread rebellion against the confines of the sentimental naturalism of the late nineteenth century—many of these posters were done by artists of real greatness like Toulouse-Lautrec and Henri Bonnard, or lesser figures like Jules Chéret (who had been inspired by American circus posters). The demand for them was at times overwhelming. People tried to steal posters or to bribe workers employed to paste them up, and art dealers found them a lucrative sideline.

Soon the "poster craze," as the phenomenon was known, had crossed the Atlantic and had America in its grip. There were poster exhibits everywhere. A bicycle manufacturer organized a mammoth competition, which brought in close to a thousand entries. Poster dealers set themselves up in almost all the major cities. Periodicals kept collectors informed on the latest poster developments. In Chicago, people gave parties at which the ladies dressed as poster figures, leaving the gentlemen to guess at their identity. In Boston, young people in love sent each other symbolic posters.

It was not that posters were new to America; the novelty was rather the poster as an art form. Since the mid-nineteenth century, posters were a common enough sight, plastered on board fences, brick walls, country barns, and covered bridges. Produced by large lithographing firms, they were the unsigned work of craftsmen who were less concerned with aesthetic theories than with the exact rendering of whatever image a client called for—whether a patent medicine remedy, a tearful scene from an Uncle Tom show, or the one and only living giraffe in America.

An exception to the rule were the posters issued by magazines in the 1880's to announce their holiday numbers. These were done by the magazines' illustrators, who traditionally signed their work. Small in format and intended for shop-window display, they were of no great

Bradley His Book

A ghostly-white maiden and a blue peacock adorned a poster by one of the best-known graphic artists of the nineties, Will H. Bradley. They advertised a short-lived magazine he edited, called—appropriately enough—Bradley, His Book.

Edward Penfield

value as works of art, being usually an enlarged illustration, fuzzily designed and overburdened with décor. Uninspired as they may have been, however, they did at least set a precedent, and gave publishers the idea of importing posters designed by leading European graphic artists of the day.

Harper's, in 1889, was the first to make the experiment, commissioning a Christmas poster by Eugene Grasset, a Swiss whose work reflected modern tastes but was not so *avant-garde* as to offend the magazine's conservative public. It was not, however, until the spring of 1893, when the poster craze on the Continent was at its height, that the editors of *Harper's* allowed one of their own artists to try a poster in the latest and most fashionable French style.

They chose a young man named Edward Penfield, who produced a design that caused a minor sensation. His work was soon so popular that during the next six years he designed a window-display poster for every issue of the magazine and became in the process the first American poster artist to win international acclaim.

Though Penfield modeled much of his work after Toulouse-Lautrec, his art was essentially American. His favorite subject was that persistent ideal of young femininity—frigidly attractive, unmistakably upper-class, slightly bored, and unassailably virginal. Penfield's maidens were either shown alone (preferably with a copy of *Harper's* held in a languid hand) or with an equally well-bred male companion indulging in seasonal pastimes—watching a horse race, sunning on the beach, riding in a carriage (they were never seen on a conveyance as bourgeois as a bicycle).

The demand for Penfield's posters was so great that often more copies of them were printed than of the magazine itself. Before long, *Harper's* competitors, the great magazines of the day like *Century* and *Scribner's*, had sensed a good thing and were issuing posters of their own. Some people even began to take the fad quite seriously and to worry, like Ruskin, about the ethical function of art in society. One popular artist, an Englishman named Louis J. Rhead, went so far as to advocate the poster as a means of uplifting the flagging moral standards of the working

Edgar Breitenbach is chief of the Prints and Photographs division of the Library of Congress. Picture credits: page 27, collection of the Coffee House Club, New York City; page 29, top center and top right, Metropolitan Museum of Art; all others, Library of Congress.

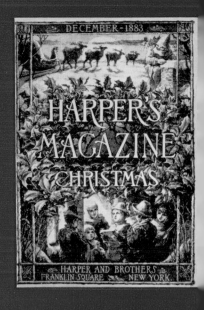

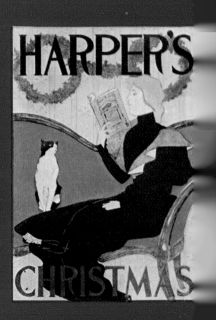

Art Nouveau
and the Magazines

Magazine and book publishers of the 1880's and 90's were responsible for making posters popular in America. The examples at left, showing the rapid development of the poster as an art form, all announced Christmas issues of Harper's. From the top are: a commonplace specimen of nineteenth-century graphic design, done in 1883; a crèche in the pre-Raphaelite manner by the eminent European poster artist Eugene Grasset, published nine years later; and an 1894 Edward Penfield creation reminiscent of the great Toulouse-Lautrec. Other mass-circulation magazines of the time were quick to follow the lead of Harper's. Century displayed a sort of art nouveau Gibson Girl by Louis J. Rhead (above), and (upper right) Lippincott's, a stylized portrayal of feminine pensiveness by Will Carqueville. At right, Maxfield Parrish's forest nymph peruses a magazine — presumably Scribner's.

Ethel Reed

classes. In his zeal to crush proletarian sensuality, Rhead took to designing impeccably moral posters of monstrous size, one of which measured twenty-four by forty-one feet.

But the craze for artistic posters might never have gained real momentum had it not been for the enthusiasm of the *avant-garde* periodicals known as "miniature" magazines. They seemed to be everywhere in the nineties, earnest and self-consciously "arty" little publications that flourished wanly for a few issues and were forgotten almost before they died. They had, in the words of H. L. Mencken, a penchant for "odd sizes, shapes, freak illustrations, wide margins, Jenson type, scurrilous abuse and petty jealousies, impossible prose and doggerel rhyme." Elbert Hubbard exaggerated only slightly when he wrote in 1896: "We now have the Lotus, the Lotos and the Lettuce. The latest is the Prairie Dog. Its hole is in Lawrence, Kansas, and it is patterned after the Chip Monk. Verily like begets like."

Actually, a few of the miniatures—the *Chap Book* of Chicago was the most notable—had real merit. Unlike the established big-circulation literary magazines, which had to be careful not to outdistance the taste of their public, the miniatures could afford to be daring—or perhaps, they could not afford to be timid. Thus their posters came to reflect the latest trends of the *art nouveau* movement; their popularity was so widespread, in fact, that in many cases the posters sold for ten times the price of the magazine.

For all its brief duration, the poster craze did produce some remarkable artists—people like Will H. Bradley, whose intricate patterns and wavy lines looked like something out of a Celtic illuminated manuscript; Ethel Reed of Boston, a young woman whose lovely poster girls were often modeled after her own stunning likeness; and John Sloan, who soon forsook the dreamlike stylization of *art nouveau* for the uncompromising realism of what came to be known as the Ashcan school.

Will H. Bradley

Like most fads, the poster craze subsided as suddenly as it had begun. By the end of 1896, one critic reported, "The absence of any new designs showing originality or uncommon merit . . . seems to prove that poster designing has seen its best days." And so, apparently, it had. As public interest waned, poster artists drifted into other fields; except for a fortunate few like Sloan or Bradley, most of them were seldom heard of again.

30

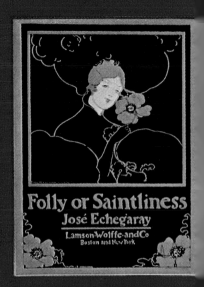

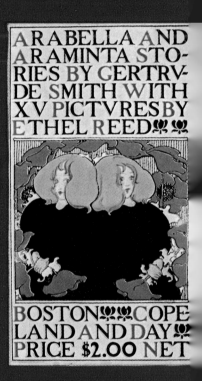

THE
ECHO

Some of the most memorable work during the brief poster fad—it was over by the turn of the century—was produced for avant-garde magazines. The Echo (left), for instance, hired a little-known artist named John Sloan, soon to become a leading spirit of the so-called Ashcan school. Two posters for one of the foremost literary periodicals of the time, The Chap Book, are reproduced at bottom—a Will H. Bradley design (left) and a carrot-haired temptress (right) by Frank Hazenplug. An amusing parody of little magazines and the posters that advertised them was produced by humorist Gelett Burgess and artist E. C. Peixotto. The spoof was called Le Petit Journal des Refusées (freely translated, "the little journal of women writers who have been turned down"); the accompanying poster depicted classic art trampled by various idols of the art nouveau movement, among them an Aubrey Beardsley lady and a Kabuki actor.

The
Passing
of a
Fancy

JOURNEY'S END: 1865

Two humble memories—a brakeman's and a carpenter's—bring back the human moments of a nation's tragedy

By WALTER HAVIGHURST

In the fall of 1864 William S. Porter, a young man from the sleepy southern Illinois town of Jerseyville, was mustered out of service with the 145th Illinois Infantry. He was just sixteen, but the war had left a man's lines in his face. A few days after his discharge he became a brakeman on the Chicago and Alton Railroad—riding on the tops of trains, setting hand brakes and couplings. From the swaying roofs of boxcars and coaches he watched the prairie roll past, in sunlight and starlight, all the way from Chicago to St. Louis. Then, one day late in April, 1865, when young Porter dropped off a train at Bloomington, Illinois, and reported to the superintendent, he found a dozen young brakemen, weathered and wind-burned like himself. They were ordered to Chicago on special duty.

On the Chicago lake front, at Twelfth Street and Michigan Avenue, Porter joined a special train, a baggage car and nine coaches, all draped in black. The first seven coaches carried a New York military company in dress uniform. The final car was occupied by an official party, including General Joseph "Fighting Joe" Hooker; Secretary of War Edwin M. Stanton; Governor Richard Yates; Captain Robert Lincoln, the late President's oldest son; and Lincoln's long-time

friend, Supreme Court Justice David Davis. The next to the last car was heavily draped in mourning, with crepe rosettes framing each of its twelve windows. On its side appeared the presidential seal, and at both vestibules stood rigid sentries wearing blue campaign caps, white gloves, and black arm bands. Within the car on a raised dais rested a small coffin containing the body of twelve-year-old Willie Lincoln, who had died three years before in Washington and was now to be buried beside his father in Springfield. There was room on the dais for a larger coffin but now that space was empty. The casket had been taken to the Chicago courthouse, where an endless stream of people passed it, night and day.

During its solemn twelve-day journey from Washington the train had been visited by thousands and seen by millions of silent people. In a dozen cities plumed horses and military companies marching to muffled drums had escorted the coffin between the cars and public buildings: Abraham Lincoln's body lay in state in the Pennsylvania Capitol at Harrisburg, in Independence Hall in Philadelphia, in the City Hall in New York—while vast, hushed crowds filed by. In Syracuse thirty thousand came through a midnight

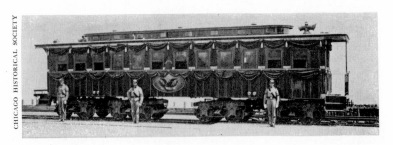

Guarded by soldiers and draped in black, the funeral car waits in the Illinois Central yards at Chicago to begin the trip to Springfield.

downpour to pay their tribute to the assassinated President. At Cleveland the bier rested in a black-draped tabernacle in the Public Square. At Columbus eight hearse horses clattered over the planking of High Street between unspeaking ranks of people, and the coffin was carried between the black-draped pillars of the Statehouse. In the rotunda over fifty thousand people, two and a half times the city's population, moved past the still figure. Indianapolis was thronged with citizens from every county of Indiana. In a steady rain, one hundred thousand awaited their turn to walk past the President's catafalque.

Abraham Lincoln's death in the hour of military triumph prevented exultation in the North; rejoicing swiftly changed to sorrow, and the whole nation bent beneath the massive tragedy of the war. In place of victory banners, every town and city hung out its emblems of grief, while bells tolled and the air shook to the somber boom of cannon.

From Washington Walt Whitman followed in his mind the President's return to the heartland.

Over the breast of the spring, the land, amid cities,
Amid lanes, and through old woods, where lately
   the violets peep'd from the ground, spotting the
   gray debris,
Amid the grass in the fields each side of the lanes,
   passing the endless grass,
Passing the yellow-spear'd wheat, every grain from its
   shroud in the dark-brown fields uprisen,
Passing the apple-tree blows of white and pink in
   the orchards,
Carrying a corpse to where it shall rest in the grave,
Night and day journeys a coffin.

In Chicago on the evening of May 2, the funeral cortege formed at Washington and LaSalle streets, outside the Cook County Courthouse. Eight sergeants carried the coffin to the hearse, drawn by eight black horses, each accompanied by a Negro groom; then the procession moved west on Madison Street with an echoing clip-clop of hooves on the pavement. Fifty thousand persons followed the military guard. More acres of people waited outside Union Station while the long coffin was carried into the train and set down again beside the small one. Night had fallen when Bill Porter freed the brakes on the funeral coach and the train began its journey back home to Springfield.

When the lights of Chicago dwindled, there remained the huge dark prairie under the stars. The train ran slow, hardly swaying on the long straight track. Lights and voices filled the cars ahead, but the funeral coach was dark and still.

Sometimes in Springfield on Sunday mornings Willie and Tad tagged along with their father to his office while their mother went to church. Willie brought his kitten. They clattered up the board stairs and into the long room with its desk, bookshelves, and paper-strewn table. They piled up books and toppled them over, they made a quiver of arrows out of pencils and a spittoon, while their father lay on the battered couch playing with the kitten. Willie was the older by three years, a bright, happy, imaginative boy who could make up games and stories. Little Thomas was a bubbler and a wriggler—"Tadpole," his father called him. When carriages passed outside, coming from church, they went home, cutting through the pasture to the sand-colored house at Eighth and Jackson streets.

In the White House in Washington Willie and Tad kept kittens, goats, rabbits, and a little dog named Jip that often sat in the President's lap at mealtimes, watchful for morsels. They had a doll named Jack, dressed like a soldier, and liable, it appeared, to stern military discipline. In their play, Jack once drew a death penalty for sleeping on picket duty. The boys dug Jack's grave in the shrubbery, but before the burial a White House gardener had an idea that the President might pardon him. The boys appealed and got a reprieve, written on Executive Mansion note paper: "The doll Jack is pardoned. By order of the President. A. Lincoln."

During the winter of 1862 Willie lay languid and bright-eyed with fever. At midnight Lincoln came in his old dressing gown and sat by the bedside, smoothing the burning forehead with his big hand. But then, in the waning light of a gray afternoon, Willie died. That evening John Nicolay found Lincoln lying on the floor of his study trying to console sobbing little Tad. Later in the war fire broke out at night in the White House stables. Lincoln ran out, asking for the horses, but was stopped by secret service men. From a bedroom window he watched the flames die down. Willie's pony was in the ruins. . . .

By midnight the whole funeral train was dark, and the rails clicked steadily under the wheels. In the catafalque car there was darkness within darkness, two coffins on the dark dais in the dark car rolling homeward over the dark prairie.

In the southern Illinois town of Alton lived Superintendent Chaffee, who had charge of bridge and carpenter work on the Chicago and Alton Railroad—nowadays the Gulf, Mobile & Ohio. One of the local boys was Edmond Beall, sixteen years old, a friend of Chaffee's son Ship. On April 19, 1865, the Superintendent rounded up his carpenters, including Ed Beall and Ship Chaffee, and left for special duty in Springfield. Half a century later Ed Beall recalled his days

On its long way home, the Lincoln train paused briefly at West Philadelphia, heading for New York. Engines were changed en route, and cars added or taken off, but the special presidential car went through. It was Mr. Lincoln's first and only trip in that overly luxurious affair, which later became a passenger coach and was destroyed by fire in 1911.

in Springfield for the Illinois State Historical Society; his letter was published in their *Journal* in 1913. Three years later Bill Porter's account of the funeral train appeared in the *Journal*. The two lads, unknown to each other, must have passed in the crowded streets of Springfield on the third and fourth days of May, 1865.

The first job was to drape the Lincoln house in mourning. Beall was a rangy youth with a long reach. When the carpenters climbed onto the steep roof of the Lincoln house, he had to hang the traditional "droopers" from the eaves above the second story. His comrades paid out a rope and Ed slid down, head first, until he could reach over the edge. When his hammer sounded, an upstairs window opened. Mrs. Lucian A. Tilton, wife of the railroad official who had rented the Lincoln house, told him to set the cloth rosettes just eight feet apart. With his head hanging into space the boy could not precisely judge that distance, and he said so. Mrs. Tilton soon reappeared with a two-foot rule taken from Lincoln's old desk. When the job was done, Ed tucked the ruler in his belt and was hauled back up the roof. For years afterward the ruler was a keepsake in the Beall house in Alton.

While the carpenters were at work, hundreds of visitors gathered at Eighth and Jackson streets. They stripped the new-leafed shrubbery for souvenirs. They hacked off splinters from the fence and dug bricks from the wall. Photographers hawked tintypes of the house, barn, and garden. Two enterprising men showed the crowd the Lincoln family horse, Old Tom, and took up a collection for their pains. Old Tom had been sold when the Lincolns left for Washington; for five years he was a familiar dray horse on the streets of Springfield. Now the two speculators had bought him for a reported five hundred dollars and were planning to take him on an exhibition tour of the country.

From the Lincoln residence the carpenters moved on to the Illinois Statehouse. They draped the building in black velvet and built a catafalque for the coffin in the Assembly Hall.

Meanwhile the crowds were growing. Every train into Springfield was crammed with visitors, and endless lines of wagons came over the Sangamon County roads. Horses, mules, traps, carts, buggies, wagons, and a multitude on foot choked the dusty streets. Old residents pointed out the Lincoln landmarks—the site of Lincoln's first law office, the room where the first county court convened, the plain Butler house where the bachelor Lincoln had lodged, the Edwards mansion where he was married, the Globe Tavern where he had taken his bride to live, the pasture where he had grazed his horse and cow.

In Washington, the distraught Mary Todd Lincoln had been unable to decide where her husband should be buried. The citizens of Springfield proposed to erect a tomb on the spacious, wooded Mather place, site of the present Illinois Capitol, on Second Street between Monroe and Edwards. Mrs. Lincoln demurred, and

One of many delegations posed before the Lincoln house, at Eighth and Jackson streets in Springfield, then occupied by the Tilton family, who had been paying the absent President $350 a year rent. Carpenter Beall's work with the mourning drapery shows clearly. The sign on the curb reads "Great Reduction/Dry Goods!"; there will always be an ad man.

while the funeral train was crossing Indiana she came to a decision. The burial should be in the Oak Ridge Cemetery on a prairie knoll beyond the northern edge of Springfield.

On the first of May, Ed Beall and the other carpenters climbed onto lumber wagons and creaked out to Oak Ridge to build a speakers' stand and seats for a three-hundred-voice choir. For two days and a night the saws and hammers sounded under the oak trees, where leaves had just begun to bud. On the morning of the third their work was done.

From Chicago the railroad officials sent orders over the line. At every creek and river, watchmen guarded the bridges. Regular trains were sent onto sidings an hour before the funeral train would pass. Two locomotives, No. 40 and No. 57, were assigned to the special train. Both were wood burners with balloon stacks, iron jackets, brass domes, brass sandboxes, and brass bell-frames—all polished like the sun. Both were decorated from the cowcatcher to the rear drawbar with flags and bunting intertwined with crepe. Under the headlight each engine carried a crayon portrait of Lincoln in a five-foot wreath of flowers. No. 40 served as a "pilot," going ahead to test the safety of the track. Veteran engineer Jim Cotton took the throttle of No. 57.

With its own slow clangor lost in the tolling of church bells, the train passed through Joliet, Wilmington, Bloomington, and Lincoln, where acres of people stood in silence. The cars crept through villages where

people had waited in the midnight hours with lanterns, flags, and torches. At every crossroad families stood bareheaded in the fitful light of bonfires. But finally sunrise warmed the prairie, and from the top of the train brakeman Porter saw the glint of water through the wooded bottoms of Salt Creek. The next downgrade carried across the Sangamon, and Springfield showed in the distance.

After all night on his carpentry job at Oak Ridge, Ed Beall climbed onto an empty lumber wagon and jolted into Springfield. The streets were filled with horses, vehicles, and people on foot—all pressing in toward the C & A depot. Three blocks north Ed jumped off the wagon and shouldered through the crowd. His workman's badge got him past the guards and onto the observation platform. He was there when the pilot engine, puffing pale woodsmoke, its brasswork gleaming under the black shroud, panted past the station. Then, while the buzzing of the crowd ceased, the funeral train steamed slowly past—the black-dressed engine, the coaches with sentries at each platform, the catafalque car with its emblems of office and of mourning. When the train stopped, the crowd surged forward. Ed Beall saw pickpockets at work below the platform. From the rear coach stepped General Joe Hooker, a straight, brisk-striding man with a face as red as an Indian's. Fighting Joe broke his stride when he saw a pickpocket reaching for a spectator's wallet. One of his feet shot out and sent the thief sprawling.

CONTINUED ON PAGE 85

"Then and there the child Independence was born"

Long before Lexington, James Otis' fight for civil liberties gave heart to the rebel cause. But why did he behave so strangely as the Revolution neared? Which side was he on?

James Otis, from the portrait by Joseph Blackburn. "I have never known a man," John Adams wrote of him, "whose love of his country was more ardent and sincere. . . ."

By RICHARD B. MORRIS

Few freedoms are more fundamental to our way of life—and few so clearly differentiate our democracy from the rival system which seeks to bury it—than the freedom from the midnight knock on the door, from the arbitrary invasion of a man's home by soldiery or police. Enshrined in the Fourth Amendment to the Constitution, the right is nevertheless still a matter of contention: almost every year that passes sees cases based upon it coming before the United States Supreme Court. Given the almost inevitable conflict between the legitimate demands of civil authority and the equally legitimate demands of individual freedom, it is likely that the controversy will be always with us.

What one famous Supreme Court justice called "the right most valued by civilized man," the right to be let alone, is a venerable one in America: long before the Revolution, violation of it by representatives of the king rankled deeply in the hearts of his American subjects; it was, indeed, one of the major reasons they eventually decided they could no longer serve him.

The issue was first expounded in the course of an extraordinary forensic argument made in the year 1761 before five scarlet-robed judges in the council chamber of the Town-house in Boston. The speaker was James Otis, Jr., then thirty-six years old, born in nearby West Barnstable and considered the ablest young lawyer at the Boston bar.

His plea for the right of privacy was at once significant and poignant. It was significant because without the burning moral issue thus precipitated, it might have been possible for the cynical to dismiss the forthcoming Revolution as a mere squabble between colonies and mother country over taxation. The poignancy of

Otis' plea derives from the brilliant young lawyer's subsequent curious conduct: while many of his friends became leaders in the fight for independence, he followed a mysterious zigzag course that unfortunately, in the eyes of some of his contemporaries, cast doubt upon his loyalty to the cause of freedom.

The specific occasion of Otis' appearance was an application to the Superior Court of Massachusetts Bay by Charles Paxton, Surveyor of Customs for the Port of Boston, for writs of assistance. These were general warrants which, as they were commonly interpreted, empowered customs officers under police protection arbitrarily to enter—if necessary, to break into—warehouses, stores, or homes to search for smuggled goods. The intruders were not even required to present any grounds for suspecting the presence of the illicit items. Such writs had been authorized in England—where they were issued by the Court of Exchequer—since the time of Charles II, but nothing like them had been used in the colonies prior to the French and Indian War. The only writs theretofore procurable had been specific search warrants issued by the regular common-law courts; but these had authorized search only in places specified in the warrants and only upon specific information, supported by oath, that smuggled goods were hidden there. True, an act of King William III regulating colonial trade had given the customs officers in America the same rights of search as their opposite numbers in England enjoyed. But it was a new question whether the royal order extended to colonial courts the same authority to issue the writs that the Court of Exchequer exercised in the mother country.

During the final phase of the Second Hundred Years' War between Britain and France, however, writs of assistance had been issued in Massachusetts to facilitate the feverish if futile efforts of customs officers to stamp out illegal trade between the colonists and the enemy—in Canada and the French West Indies. These writs had been issued in the name of King George II, but that monarch died in October, 1760, and his grandson succeeded to the throne as George III. According to law, the old writs expired six months after the death of a sovereign, and new ones had to be issued in the name of his successor. Now, in February of 1761, while the issue hung in the balance—George III would not be crowned until September—Surveyor Paxton's case came to trial.

Sixty-three prominent Boston merchants joined to oppose him, retaining the brilliant, impassioned, unstable Otis—and his amiable and temperate associate, Oxenbridge Thacher—to represent them. In order to take their case, Otis resigned his office as Advocate General of the Vice-Admiralty Court, in which capacity he would have been expected to represent the Crown and present the other side of the argument. That task was now assigned to Jeremiah Gridley, a leader of the Boston bar, who appeared as counsel for the customs officers.

Behind Otis' resignation lay deep personal animosities that added drama to the legal battle. Not long before, the chief justiceship of the Superior Court—which would hear the arguments on the writs of assistance and render a decision—had fallen vacant. William Shirley, then governor of the colony, had promised the post to Otis' father, but Shirley's successor, Francis Bernard, had ignored the commitment and instead named his lieutenant governor, Thomas Hutchinson. Already the target of colonists who resented his nepotistic use of the lieutenant governorship, Hutchinson now earned additional criticism for holding two offices at the same time. And his appointment of course precipitated a feud with the influential Otises; young James, according to rumor, declared "he would set the province in flames, if he perished by the fire."

Nevertheless Hutchinson, attired in his new judicial robes, took his seat in the great Town-house council chamber as the trial opened on February 24. With him on the bench were Justices Lynde, Cushing, Oliver, and Russell. Gridley opened for the Crown. He argued that such general writs were being issued in England by the Court of Exchequer, which had the statutory authority to issue them; the province law of 1699, he continued, had granted the Superior Court jurisdiction in Massachusetts "generally" over matters which the courts of King's Bench, Common Pleas, and Exchequer "have or ought to have."

Thacher replied first. Addressing himself largely to technical issues, he denied that the Superior Court could exercise the right of the Court of Exchequer in England to issue such writs. Then Otis arose to speak. One contemporary critic described him as "a plump, round-faced, smooth skinned, short-necked, eagle-eyed politician," but to John Adams—who attended the trial, reported it in his diary, and was to write an account of it more than fifty years later—"Otis was a flame of fire."

He had prepared his argument with care. Although his oration covered some four or five hours and was not taken down stenographically, it left on Adams an indelible impression. With a "profusion of legal authorities," Adams tells us, "a prophetic glance of his eye into futurity, and a torrent of impetuous eloquence, he hurried away everything before him." Adams continued: "Every man of a crowded audience appeared to me to go away, as I did, ready to take arms against writs of assistance." And he concluded: "Then and there the child Independence was born."

More important than the electrifying effect of Otis' argument upon his auditors was its revolutionary tenor. Anticipating ideas that would be set forth in the Declaration of Independence fifteen years later, Otis argued that the rights to life, liberty, and property were derived from nature and implied the guarantee of privacy, without which individual liberty could not survive. (Venturing beyond the immediate issue, Otis declared that liberty should be granted to all men regardless of color—an abolitionist note that startled even the sympathetic Adams.)

Relying on English lawbooks to prove that only special warrants were legal, Otis attacked the writs as "instruments of slavery," which he swore to oppose to his dying day with all the powers and faculties God had given him. Defending the right of privacy, he pointed out that the power to issue general search warrants placed "the liberty of every man in the hands of every petty officer." The freedom of one's house, he contended, was "one of the most essential branches of English liberty." In perhaps his most moving passage he was reported to have declared:

A man's house is his castle, and whilst he is quiet he is as well guarded as a prince in his castle. This writ, if it should be declared legal, would totally annihilate this privilege. Custom-house officers may enter our houses when they please; we are commanded to permit their entry. Their menial servants may enter, may break locks, bars, and everything in their way; and whether they break through malice or revenge, no man, no court, can inquire. Bare suspicion without oath is sufficient. This wanton exercise of this power is not a chimerical suggestion of a heated brain. . . . What a scene does this open! Every man, prompted by revenge, ill humor, or wantonness to inspect the inside of his neighbor's house, may get a writ of assistance. Others will ask it from self-defense; one arbitrary exertion will provoke another, until society be involved in tumult and blood.

With remarkable prescience Otis' words captured the mood of the midnight visitation by totalitarian police which would terrify a later era less sensitive to individual freedom.

Otis then proceeded to denounce the Navigation Acts, which had regulated the trade of the empire since the time of Cromwell, exposing their nuisance aspects with great wit. By implication he acknowledged the widespread existence of smuggling, and went so far as to contend that "if the King of Great Britain in person were encamped on Boston Common, at the head of twenty thousand men, with all his navy on our coast, he would not be able to execute these laws. They would be resisted or eluded." Turning to the similarly unenforceable Molasses Act, passed by Parliament in 1733 to protect the British West Indies planters from the competition of the foreign West Indies, he charged that the law was enacted "by a foreign legislature, without our consent, and by a legislature who had no feeling for us, and whose interest prompted them to tax us to the quick."

The nub of Otis' argument was that, even if the writs of assistance had been authorized by an Act of Parliament, "an act against the Constitution is void. An act against natural equity is void; and if an act of Parliament should be made, in the very words of this petition, it would be void. The executive courts * must pass such acts into disuse." This contention—that Parliament was not omnipotent and could be restrained by the unwritten Constitution and a higher law—was a notion soon to be pushed further by John Adams and other members of the Massachusetts bar; the argument became familiar in the colonies well before the Declaration of Independence was adopted.

Measured by its effect on its auditors and its immediate impact on the majority of the court, Otis' speech ranks among the most memorable in American history, alongside Patrick Henry's fiery oration protesting the Stamp Act, Fisher Ames' memorable defense of Jay's Treaty in the House of Representatives, and Daniel Webster's classic reply to Hayne. Had a decision been rendered on the spot, Otis and Thacher would have won, for all the judges save Thomas Hutchinson were against the writs; even from *his* opinion, carefully worded, opponents of the writs could take comfort: "The Court has considered the subject of writs of assistance," the chief justice announced, "and can see no foundation for such a writ; but as the practice in England is not known [owing to the interregnum], it has been thought best to continue the question to the next term, and that in the meantime opportunity may be given to know the result." But the crafty chief justice, aware that he stood alone among his colleagues, was merely buying precious time.

Another hearing was held in November, 1761. This time Robert Auchmuty joined Gridley in defense of the writs. The arguments lasted "the whole day and evening," covering much the same ground as the previous hearing. But the court had now before it information that under the new monarch, George III, writs of assistance were being issued in the mother country by the Court of Exchequer; the Massachusetts judges accordingly felt that they could no longer refuse to issue them too. Writing years later, John Adams re-

* By "executive courts" he meant the regular courts of law as distinguished from the Massachusetts legislature, known as the General Court. Otis' argument presaged a special and unique role for the United States Supreme Court, the exercise of the power to declare laws unconstitutional.

counted that "the Court clandestinely granted them."

Thomas Hutchinson had won a pyrrhic victory. It was he who had talked the rest of the court into agreeing to a delay to learn what the English practice was and he who was chiefly responsible for granting the writs. He was to pay dearly in personal popularity. Moreover, at the younger Otis' prompting, the legislature manifested its displeasure with the decision not only by reducing the salary of the judges of the Superior Court, but by cutting out entirely Hutchinson's allowance as chief justice. And that was only the beginning. During the riots in Boston in 1765 over the passage of the Stamp Act, Hutchinson's mansion was sacked and his library and papers scattered—out of revenge, Governor Bernard claimed, for his connection with the writs. Henceforward, Hutchinson was to be the leader of the Court party and a frank advocate of coercion to secure colonial obedience to Parliament.

As for James Otis, his initial attack upon the writs had made him the darling of the populace of Boston and the leader of the radical party. Taking the issue to the people at once—in May of 1761—he won election to the Massachusetts General Court. When the news of it reached Worcester, Brigadier Timothy Ruggles, then chief justice of the common pleas court and later a Tory exile, declared at a dinner party in John Adams' presence, "Out of this election will arise a damned faction, which will shake this province to its foundation."

Ruggles' gloomy forebodings proved even more accurate than he could have expected, for the year 1761 triggered the Revolutionary movement, and the Otises, father and son, set off the chain reaction. That same year the father was re-elected Speaker of the House. Together they succeeded in pushing through an act forbidding the courts to issue any writ that did not specify under oath the person and place to be searched. On the advice of the justices of the Superior Court, Governor Bernard refused to approve the legislation; overoptimistically he stigmatized it as a "last effort of the confederacy against the customhouse and laws of trade."

The constitutional views which Otis first expounded in the writs of assistance case were given more elaborate formulation in a forceful political tract, "A Vindication of the Conduct of the House of Representatives," which he published in 1762. Therein he enunciated the Whig view that all men are naturally equal, and that kings are made to serve the people, not people the ends of kings.

It would be gratifying to report that the man who had made a political career out of his opposition to the writs was in the forefront of the Revolution when the fighting actually got under way. Regrettably, he

was not. Quick-tempered and tense, increasingly eccentric and even abusive, Otis simply was not cast in the heroic mold. Whether from self-interest, fear, expediency, irresponsibility, or family friction (his wife was a high Tory and a shrew), or from a combination of all five, Otis now followed a vacillating course that branded him a recreant to his own principles, loathed by his foes, deserted by his followers.

It all started with what looked suspiciously like a deal. In 1764 Governor Bernard appointed Otis Senior chief justice of the Court of Common Pleas and judge of probate in Barnstable County. In that same year the son issued his "Rights of the British Colonies Asserted and Proved," the most influential American pamphlet published prior to John Dickinson's "Letters from a Farmer in Pennsylvania." Written in opposition to the Sugar Act, Otis' tract took the position that Parliament had no right to tax the colonies and that taxation was "absolutely irreconcilable" with the rights of the colonists as British subjects—indeed, as human beings. Nevertheless, it gave comfort to the Court party by affirming the subordination of the colonies to Great Britain and the right of Parliament to legislate for them in matters other than taxation. Hailed by the Whigs in England, the pamphlet elicited a grudging compliment from Lord Mansfield, who quickly pounced on Otis' concession of the supremacy of the Crown. When someone said that Otis was mad, Mansfield rejoiced that in all popular assemblies "madness is catching." The evidence that the younger Otis' more con-

CONTINUED ON PAGE 82

MASSACHUSETTS HISTORICAL SOCIETY

Leader of the Court party and Otis' implacable foe was Chief Justice Thomas Hutchinson.

This portrait of George W. Perkins was painted at his Riverdale, New York, home by Soralla in 1909.

The Millionaire Reformer

*In the era of the Bull Moose, Progressivism became a party;
the man behind Roosevelt was, of all things, a Morgan partner*

By JOHN A. GARRATY

It is the evening of June 20, 1912; the scene, a large room in the Congress Hotel in Chicago. About twenty men are present. Perhaps a dozen of them are seated around a large table. Others sprawl wearily in armchairs or lean against the walls. One, a solid, determined-looking fellow with thick glasses and a bristling mustache, paces grimly back and forth in silence, like a caged grizzly. He is Theodore Roosevelt, and these are his closest political advisers. All of them are very, very angry.

In a nearby auditorium, the Republican National Convention is moving with the ponderous certainty of a steamroller toward the nomination of well-fed William Howard Taft for a second term as President of the United States. All of the men in the hotel room believe that this nomination rightfully belongs to Roosevelt, and that it is being "stolen" by a cynical band of reactionary politicians who have used their control of the party machinery to seat enough illegally chosen delegates to insure the selection of their man Taft. The Roosevelt men do not want to take this lying down; they would like to run their candidate on a third-party ticket. But they realize that without a great deal of money such a plan would be impossible. Frustration thus feeds and intensifies their anger.

It is growing late, and everyone is weary. Conversation lags. But gradually attention is centered on two men who have withdrawn to a corner. They are talking excitedly in rapid whispers. One is the publisher Frank Munsey; the other, George W. Perkins, a former partner in J. P. Morgan & Company. Neither has had much political experience, but both are very rich and very fond of Theodore Roosevelt. Now everyone senses their subject and realizes its importance. All eyes are focused in their direction. Suddenly the two millionaires reach a decision. They straighten up and stride across the room to Roosevelt. Each places a hand on one of his shoulders. "Colonel," they say simply, "we will see you through." Thus the Progressive party— "Bull Moose," some will call it—is born.

Of these two, Munsey has relatively little importance in the story of modern American reform. He was neither entirely in sympathy with Progressive aims nor even particularly interested in them. His attachment to Roosevelt was personal, and it did not last much beyond the 1912 campaign. Perkins, however, went on to become a central figure in the history of the Progressive movement.

A central figure, but not a typical one, for no single human being can be said to represent fully that multi-faceted, contradictory, and disorganized mass drive for change. For example, Perkins was not, like William Jennings Bryan, the representative of disgruntled farmers frightened by loss of status and the rise of giant corporations, nor was he, like Roosevelt, an aristocrat striking out at the crass commercialism of the new industrial tycoons. Indeed, he was part of the new power elite that the Bryans, born poor, and Roosevelts, born rich, found so offensive and incomprehensible in the Progressive era. But Perkins was a businessman with a highly developed social conscience and a feeling that the times called for change if past progress was to continue in the future. This, certainly, was characteristically "Progressive." Without accepting the arguments of the socialists, he had learned not to be afraid of government regulation or of the thought of "tampering" with the economy.

In the early years of this century many businessmen also shared this general point of view. But most confined their political activities to signing checks at campaign time; few were willing or able to put aside money-making, climb up on a soapbox, and campaign among the politicians and plain people for what they thought was right. Perkins did these things. He paid a high price, and not only in money, but he did not mind; he had the spirit of the crusader. This, too, was typically "Progressive."

Nevertheless, in 1912 many people, including some of those in Roosevelt's hotel room in Chicago, considered Perkins utterly out of place in such a gathering of advanced liberals. They knew him as the right-hand man of the hated plutocrat J. P. Morgan; as a slick, smooth-talking apologist for monopolistic corporations like U.S. Steel and International Harvester; as a powerful insurance executive whose "crimes" had been "exposed" by Charles Evans Hughes in the famous Armstrong insurance investigation of 1905.* With his handsome, clean-cut features, his wavy brown hair only beginning to be flecked with gray at the temples, and his trim mustache, he looked too much like what in fact he had been: a typical boy wonder of Wall Street. This man was many times a millionaire while scarcely forty—a driving, aggressive manager of men and money. He owned a palatial estate, Glyndor, overlooking the Hudson at Riverdale; he belonged to the New York Yacht Club and other exclusive organizations. What was *Perkins* doing posing as a reformer, associating with a liberal like Teddy Roosevelt?

Actually, Perkins was perfectly sincere in his Progressivism. As we shall see, he did have serious personal weaknesses as a political leader, but this suspicion of his motives reflects only the confusion, jealousy, fanaticism, and small-mindedness of other Progressive reformers. Fifty years old in 1912, he had begun his career at fifteen as a $25-a-month office boy in the vast corporate anthill of the New York Life Insurance Company. Although he lacked even the beginning of a high school education, he had demonstrated powers of salesmanship and management that won him a vice-presidency at thirty.

* The charges were later dismissed in a federal court after the politicking was over.

From insurance he moved on to corporate finance. So engaging and convincing was his personality that Pierpont Morgan offered him a partnership worth millions the first time they met. As right-hand man to Morgan, Perkins supervised the organization of the Northern Securities Company (the first great corporation attacked by Roosevelt under the Sherman Antitrust Act). He wrested control of the Louisville and Nashville Railroad from the grasp of John W. "Bet-you-a-million" Gates. He represented Morgan at the White House conference where the great coal strike of 1902 was settled. He was in the thick of the fight in which Morgan stopped the Wall Street panic of 1907, and he was Morgan's man in U.S. Steel, where for years he was chairman of the all-powerful finance committee (*see* "Charlie Schwab Breaks the Bank," and "A Lion in the Street," AMERICAN HERITAGE, April and June, 1957).

In 1902 Perkins also created the agricultural machinery "trust," the International Harvester Company. In a brilliant maneuver he brought the principal owners of the four leading companies manufacturing farm machinery to New York. All of these men favored a merger, but personal rivalries in the intensely competitive harvester business had frustrated all their efforts to work out an agreement. Installing each group in a different hotel to discourage them from seeing one another, Perkins scurried back and forth settling the details of the new combination. Such was the eventual confidence of all parties in his fairness that when the final critical allotment of stock in the new corporation was made, the heads of the four companies simply signed their names to this statement addressed to Perkins: "We place in your hands the final determination of our appraisal values, special good will, scaling, etc., etc." McCormicks and Deerings held the top offices, but Perkins was the real manager of the destinies of International Harvester for many years. It was prizes like this, the not unrewarded amenities of a partnership in the House of Morgan, that Perkins gave up when he set out as a crusader for reform.

Was it really so surprising? Perkins had always possessed, or, if you will, suffered from, a "do-good" streak. His father, an insurance man also, had been a social worker deeply involved in the management of boys' reform schools. He developed in young George an interest in the Y.M.C.A. and in various religious organizations. To the Perkins family, selling insurance had been a way of performing a useful social service as well as making a good livelihood. Later, when Morgan first offered him the prospect of great wealth if he would enter the firm, Perkins actually turned him down. Only when the banker described the opportunities that the job would offer for dealing with the complex social and economic questions posed by the rise of giant corporations did Perkins lend a sympathetic ear.

Perkins' experience in managing large businesses gave him a special interest in labor relations. At New York Life he had developed a pension and profit-sharing program for agency directors and salesmen. This program he greatly expanded in the steel and harvester companies. Recognizing long before the idea was common that the lack of contact and understanding between worker and employer was a prime cause of bad labor relations in big corporations, he tried to interest workers in buying stock in the companies that employed them. He developed a plan for U.S. Steel whereby a worker who invested $82.50 in a share of Steel Preferred cleared $125.04 in five years—and still owned the stock. Critics on the left charged that this was a subtle way of preventing the growth of unions. Perkins rejected the unions' basic belief that there was a fundamental conflict of interest between capital and labor, but he was not unsympathetic to organized labor. At one point he suggested that a steelworker should be on the Board of Directors; it was all very advanced for the time.

The new reformer's labors with giants like New York Life and U.S. Steel had convinced him that mere bigness in business was not a crime, as the "trust busters" were arguing, but a necessity. The savings resulting from large-scale operation, the ability to take the long-range view, to plan, to engage in expensive research —these made the large corporation efficient and hence socially desirable. Competition, the law of tooth and claw, was crude, cruel, uncivilized, Perkins believed. Antitrust laws were out of date; instead of breaking up the giants, government should simply regulate their activities. Modern technology and mass markets were making older forms of business organization obsolete. Instead of competition, co-operation should be the byword of the modern world. Perkins believed that large corporations, with their thousands of stockholders, were truly "public" businesses. The function of corporate managers like himself, he said in a lecture at Columbia University in 1908, was to decide "what is fair and right between the public's capital, which they represent, and the public's labor, which they employ."

Beginning early in 1911, Perkins devoted most of his time to advocating these ideas. He accepted speaking engagements all over the country and wrote unceasingly on the subject. Inevitably his crusade involved him in politics, although he had not conceived of becoming a politician when he cut loose from his business ties.

Perkins had always been a Republican. As late as 1908 he had worked actively for William Howard Taft against Bryan. But after 1910 he became increasingly dismayed by Taft's attitude toward big business. Although the President allied himself generally with the conservatives, he was a confirmed trust buster. "We must get back to competition," he said. "If it is impossible, then let us go on to socialism, for there is no way between." Perkins was convinced that there was a "way between": regulation of large corporations by the federal government. When Taft ordered antitrust suits against both U.S. Steel and International Harvester, Perkins went definitely into the opposition. Like most liberal Republicans, he thought Roosevelt the most attractive alternative.

Despite his lack of political experience, Perkins became chairman of the new Progressive or "Bull Moose" party's executive committee. In effect he was Roosevelt's campaign manager, and he tried to run the campaign the way an insurance man conducts a drive for new business. To him, voters were like the policyholders and "prospects" of the insurance world. One of the Progressive party's great handicaps was that it had only "prospects" at the moment, and so a great sales campaign commenced.

Directing the fight from New York headquarters, Perkins was soon flooding the mails with torrents of campaign literature. Three million copies of Roosevelt's "Confession of Faith" were distributed. Countless other pamphlets followed. Perkins established a weekly magazine called the *Progressive Bulletin,* copied from a bulletin he had edited for years while working for New York Life. Like its prototype, it was full of slogans designed to inspire confidence in the faithful, along with "up-to-date, sledge-hammer arguments" to convince the doubtful. "What are you doing to help the Progressive party? Are you telling our story to every man and woman you meet?" Under Perkins the political "hard sell" reached a new peak.

It made for an exciting and hard-fought, if inevitably unsuccessful, effort. The fundamental fact of 1912 was that the Republicans had split while the Democrats remained united. Had the Democrats nominated a conservative like Champ Clark of Missouri, who almost won out at their convention, Roosevelt might have been elected, for 1912 marked the high-water mark of the Progressive wave. But with Woodrow Wilson in the fight, fresh from his triumphs as Governor of New Jersey, Progressives could choose between two appealing candidates. Wilson collected his

CONTINUED ON PAGE 86

The New   Portland Sun.

A remarkable group of photographs preserves the memory
of a vigorous rural people—and a quite vanished world

The FACE *of* MAINE

It used to be, in the not-so-long-ago, that the faces of Americans were richly varied. At a glance, farmers could be distinguished from city folk, mountaineers from plainsmen, easterners from westerners. Something—the gradual assimilation of the immigrants, the quickening flight from countryside to city, standardization of dress, the ubiquity of television—has changed all that. In appearance we are becoming, like the morning milk, homogenized.

It is refreshing, therefore, to look into the faces of our forebears—not only at those who became rich and famous, but at ordinary people who grew up, fell in love and founded families, tamed the land, and—if they were lucky—saw their children's children unto the third generation. Such are the faces that make up the portfolio beginning here. These are down-Easters, citizens of rural Maine, two generations ago. The pictures were taken by an unusually gifted photographer, Chansonetta Stanley Emmons, who looks out at us from the self-portrait above (it was made with the aid of a mirror). Beginning in the 1880's in her native village of Kingfield, she took her cumbersome box-type camera into blacksmith shop (left) and gristmill, barn and farmyard, kitchen and parlor, to photograph her friends and neighbors. The little girl with her admirer on page 50 is her daughter Dorothy; the demure young lady opposite, her niece Blanche.

From her famous twin brothers, who would one day build the wonderful Stanley Steamer, Mrs. Emmons received priceless aid: about the time she began taking pictures, they developed a successful dry-plate process which freed her from the confining walls of a studio and enabled her to concentrate on subject, lighting, and composition. The results were remarkable: not only did she record a set of strong, distinctive faces; she also preserved on glass plates—now owned by her son-in-law, Irl G. Whitchurch—a now-forgotten way of life.

CHILDHOOD

COURTING

OVERLEAF:

At the Blacksmith's

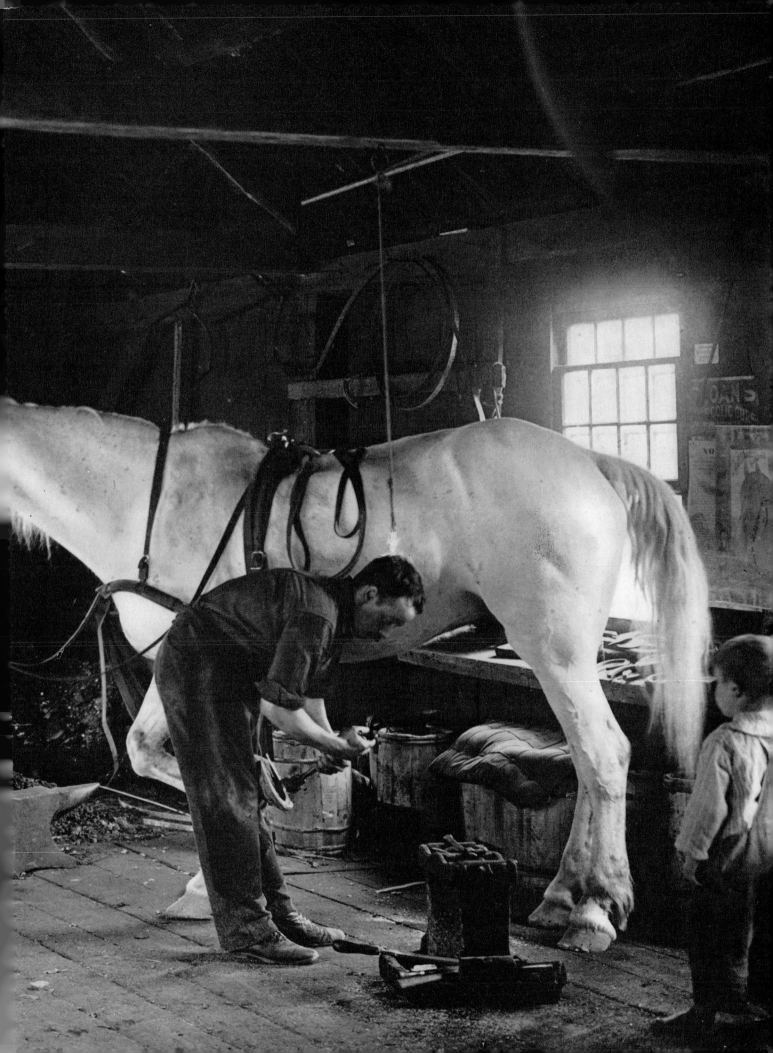

OLD AGE

In Grant Wood's affectionate satire of the cherry tree tale, called Parson Weems' Fable, *young Washington, supposedly then six, has the face of his most popular likeness, the Gilbert Stuart portrait; Weems, at the curtain, wears a proud author's faint smile. The painting dates from the late 1930's; even then, however, the true believers were scandalized by Wood's impiety.*

THE *L*EGEND MAKER

For Mason Locke Weems, ex-parson, book salesman, and moralist, tract-writing and biography were all the same thing. George Washington's image has yet to recover

By DAVID D. VAN TASSEL

There is no more famous American legend than the story of George Washington and the cherry tree that first appeared in 1806 in a little book on Washington by Mason Locke Weems. According to Weems, one day little George, armed with a new hatchet, "unluckily tried the edge . . . on the body of a beautiful young English cherry-tree, which he barked . . . terribly." The next morning his father discovered the tragedy, and the "old gentleman" demanded "with much warmth" the name of the culprit.

"George," said his father, "do you know who killed that beautiful little cherry tree yonder in the garden?" This was a *tough question;* and George staggered under it for a moment; but quickly recovered himself: and looking at his father, with the sweet face of youth brightened with the inexpressible charm of all-conquering truth, he bravely cried out, "I can't tell a lie, Pa; you know I can't tell a lie. I did cut it with my hatchet."—"Run to my arms, you dearest boy," cried his father in transports, "run to my arms; glad am I, George, that you killed my tree; for you have paid me for it a thousand fold."

Thus George escaped a whipping, the country gained a national legend, and parents were armed with an impeccable example of honesty, the purpose which the author hoped it would serve. This story for decades has been the favorite target of debunkers and sophisticates; yet it is the most durable of Weems' anecdotes about Washington, and no scholar has succeeded in proving it false. Generations of Americans, if they knew little else about their heritage, knew that George Washington never lied and that he was the brave, honorable, and supremely virtuous father of his country —the portrait that Weems created. For decades teachers, historians, and biographers have labored, largely in vain, to substitute a more lifelike and credible image in the public mind and to lay forever some of the apocryphal anecdotes related by the good Parson Weems.

Whether George actually cut down the cherry tree or not is of little consequence; but the fact that the story endures, along with the image of our first President that Parson Weems popularized, tells a great deal about the character of the American people then and now. In order to understand a little better the durability of the legend, one must become acquainted with Mason Locke Weems, his times, his people, and his work. Weems did a far greater service to his country than simply originating a famous anecdote. He created a national symbol and a model hero for a democracy.

At the time Parson Weems wrote his life of Washington (1799–1800), the United States was sixteen years old and had survived just ten years under the Constitution. The new republic was still an unproven experiment in democracy, and many thoughtful men doubted that it would survive much longer as a single nation. States boldly continued to question the sovereignty of the federal government, and at times even threatened secession. There was no national literature, no common heritage except that of England, which had been renounced. Congressmen still had difficulty acting as servants of a nation rather than as delegates to an international conference. Men still referred to their state as their "country." State historians were busily bolstering local loyalty with formal histories, claiming a full share of the glories won by native sons. Virginia was about to reclaim Washington as a state hero, but Parson Weems, by virtue of writing the first biography, and by far the most popular one, insured that Washington would remain forever an American first, a Virginian second.

Mason Locke Weems' motives for writing were not, however, overwhelmingly patriotic. One day in June, 1799, he wrote a letter to his employer, the prominent Philadelphia publisher Mathew Carey. The Reverend Mr. Weems, an irrepressibly jocular minister-turned-book-peddler and an ardent admirer of the dollar, had a scheme. "I have nearly ready for the press," he reported eagerly, "a piece christen^d, or to be christen^d, 'The Beauties of Washington.' 'Tis artfully drawn up, enliven^d with anecdotes, and in my humble opinion, marvellously fitted, 'ad captandum—gustum populi Americani!!!!' What say you to printing it . . . ?"

Here for the first time Weems mentioned the project that was to rocket him to fame if not to fortune. When he planned his book, Washington was very much alive, living in uneasy retirement at Mount Vernon and expecting momentarily to be called back to the service of his country should the current diplomatic crisis between France and the United States end in war. The irreverent little Parson saw in the ex-President's continued popularity a chance to make some money. In the same letter Weems suggested that Carey decorate the proposed volume with a copperplate frontispiece of "that Heroe," under which might be engraved, he advised, "something in this way. George Washington Esqr. The Guardian Angel of his Country. 'Go thy way old George. Die when thou wilt we shall never look upon thy like again.'" To clinch his case, Weems scrawled a postscript assuring Carey that "it

CONTINUED ON PAGE 89

Longfellow and
The Jewish Cemetery at Newport

In the summer of 1852 Henry Wadsworth Longfellow, vacationing with his family in Newport, Rhode Island, happened one day upon the old Jewish cemetery, established in 1677. Impressed by the quiet of the ancient burial ground amid the bustle of the busy seaport, he persuaded "Mr. Gould the Tailor, a polite old gentleman who keeps the key," to admit him into its silent serenity. The now-famous poem at right resulted from his walk among the crumbling tombstones.

Isaacs, Judah, Moses, Alvares, Rivera—these first Jews of Newport had arrived in the New World in 1658, fleeing religious persecution. The settlement of Newport, then only nineteen years old, welcomed them—and, later, a group of Spanish-Portuguese Jews who fled the Inquisition.

In 1759 Newport's Jewish community built one of the first synagogues in the New World, naming it Touro for its first rabbi, whose descendants lie buried beneath the graceful monuments on the opposite page. They, and the humbler Jews whose names adorn the more modest graves on the following pages, repose in surroundings little changed since Longfellow found them "at rest in all this moving up and down." But their dead nation, contrary to Longfellow's expectations and in a manner beyond his ken, would rise again.

Text and photographs by Irving Fitzig

How strange it seems! These Hebrews in their graves,
Close by the street of this fair seaport town,
Silent beside the never-silent waves,
At rest in all this moving up and down!

The trees are white with dust, that o'er their sleep
Wave their broad curtains in the southwind's breath,
While underneath these leafy tents they keep
The long, mysterious Exodus of Death.

And these sepulchral stones, so old and brown,
That pave with level flags their burial-place,
Seem like the tablets of the Law, thrown down
And broken by Moses at the mountain's base.

The very names recorded here are strange,
Of foreign accent, and of different climes;
Alvares and Rivera interchange
With Abraham and Jacob of old times.

'Blessed be God, for he created Death!'
The mourners said, 'and Death is rest and peace';
Then added, in the certainty of faith,
'And giveth Life that nevermore shall cease.'

Closed are the portals of their Synagogue,
No Psalms of David now the silence break,
No Rabbi reads the ancient Decalogue
In the grand dialect the Prophets spake.

Gone are the living, but the dead remain,
And not neglected; for a hand unseen,
Scattering its bounty, like a summer rain,
Still keeps their graves and their remem-
*   brance green.*

How came they here? What burst of Chris-
*   tian hate,*
What persecution, merciless and blind,
Drove o'er the sea—that desert desolate—
These Ishmaels and Hagars of mankind?

They lived in narrow streets and lanes
*   obscure,*
Ghetto and Judenstrass, in mirk and mire;
Taught in the school of patience to endure
The life of anguish and the death of fire.

All their lives long, with the unleavened
*   bread*
And bitter herbs of exile and its fears,
The wasting famine of the heart they fed,
And slaked its thirst with marah of their
*   tears.*

Anathema maranatha! was the cry
That rang from town to town, from street
    to street:
At every gate the accursed Mordecai
Was mocked and jeered, and spurned by
    Christian feet.

Pride and humiliation hand in hand
Walked with them through the world
    where'er they went;
Trampled and beaten were they as the
    sand,
And yet unshaken as the continent.

For in the background figures vague and vast
Of patriarchs and of prophets rose sublime,
And all the great traditions of the Past
They saw reflected in the coming time.

And thus forever with reverted look
The mystic volume of the world they read,
Spelling it backward, like a Hebrew book,
Till life became a Legend of the Dead.

But ah! what once has been shall be no
    more!
The groaning earth in travail and in pain
Brings forth its races, but does not restore,
And the dead nations never rise again.

Though war with Japan was expected momentarily, and four carriers of the Imperial Navy were ominously unaccounted for, no one thought to protect our most important Pacific base from surprise attack. Why?

Pearl Harbor:
WHO BLUNDERED?

By COLONEL T. N. DUPUY

Precisely at 7:55 A.M. on Sunday, December 7, 1941, a devastating Japanese aerial attack struck the island of Oahu, Territory of Hawaii. When it was over, the battleships of our Pacific Fleet, moored by pairs in their Pearl Harbor base, had received a mortal blow. Our army air strength in Hawaii—the Japanese found its planes ranged neatly wing to wing on airfield ramps—was a tangled mass of smoking wreckage.

The worst disaster in the military annals of the United States had ushered us into World War II. As in most wars, the political and diplomatic background was so complex and confused as to defy definitive analysis—though this has not prevented historians and others from making the attempt. But as to the disaster itself, the military record is clear.

A well-planned and brilliantly executed surprise attack by Japanese carrier-based aircraft was launched against the major American bastion in the Pacific. The United States government, its senior military leaders, and its commanders in Hawaii had had sufficient information to be adequately warned that an attack was possible, and had had time to be prepared to thwart or to blunt the blow. The information was largely ignored; the preparations were utterly inadequate.

Someone had blundered. Who? And how?

Peacetime deck awnings were still in place when Japanese torpedoes breached the hull of the U.S.S. California. Here, minutes after the attack, rescue launches rush to evacuate the crew of the sinking battleship.

At the moment of the attack four professional military men filled posts of vital importance. In Washington, General George C. Marshall, Chief of Staff, was responsible for the entire United States Army and all of its installations. In a nearby office sat his Navy counterpart, Admiral Harold R. Stark, Chief of Naval Operations. On the Hawaiian island of Oahu, Lieutenant General Walter C. Short commanded the Hawaiian Department, the Army's most vital overseas outpost. Commanding the United States Pacific Fleet was Rear Admiral Husband E. Kimmel; his headquarters was also on Oahu, overlooking the great Navy base at Pearl Harbor.

Marshall, product of the Virginia Military Institute, had a well-deserved reputation for brilliant staff work under Pershing in France in World War I. Later he had taken a prominent part in developing the Army's Infantry School at Fort Benning, Georgia. Short, a graduate of the University of Illinois, had entered the Army from civilian life in 1901. Early in 1941 he had been chosen by Marshall to command the Hawaiian Department.

Both Stark and Kimmel had graduated from the United States Naval Academy at Annapolis—Stark in 1903, Kimmel a year later. Both had risen to their high positions in the Navy following exemplary command and staff service at sea and on shore. Close personal friends, both were highly respected by their naval colleagues.

The thinking and attitudes of these four men were shaped by

ILLUSTRATED FOR AMERICAN HERITAGE BY JOSEPH PAPIN

two decades of unanimous opinion among American soldiers and sailors that someday Japan would clash with the United States in a struggle for predominance in the vast Pacific Ocean. All accepted without question the basic elements of U.S. doctrine for the defense of the Pacific in such a war.

The doctrine was that the United States Navy—and in particular its Pacific Fleet—was the essential element to American success in a Pacific war. Immobilization or destruction of that fleet would be the greatest damage Japan could inflict on the United States. Upon the Army lay the responsibility for furthering the offensive powers of the fleet by protecting its great Pearl Harbor base; by safeguarding the Panama Canal, the Navy's life line from the Atlantic to the Pacific; and by defending the advanced Philippine delaying position, which in military opinion was likely to be Japan's initial target.

Since 1939 the top military authorities of the nation, including President Franklin D. Roosevelt, had understood the almost inexorable logic of events that pointed to our eventual involvement either in the conflict which Hitler had begun in Europe or that in Asia between Japan and China—or both. And under Roosevelt's skillful guidance the nation, albeit grudgingly, was very slowly building up its military strength.

As 1941 rolled along, it became apparent, even to the man in the street, that the most pressing danger lay in the Far East. Our diplomatic relations with Japan were worsening; by November they appeared to be almost at the breaking point. The long-continued diplomatic bickering between the two nations on a variety of subjects had resulted in the arrival in Washington of a special envoy, Saburo Kurusu, who—with Ambassador Kichisaburo Nomura—had on November 20 presented the State Department with a document that was practically an ultimatum.

Japan would acquiesce to our government's demands that she withdraw from Indochina only upon "estab-

lishment of an equitable peace in the Pacific area" and, further, upon "supply to Japan [by the U.S. of] a required quantity of oil."

In 1940, our cipher experts had cracked the Japanese secret codes—a cryptoanalytical procedure known in the War Department as "Magic." Hence our government knew that the envoys had received instructions to press for American acceptance of this "final proposal" by November 25. The ambassadors had been warned that for reasons "beyond your ability to guess" this was essential, but that if the "signing can be completed by the 29th" the Imperial Japanese government would wait. "After that things are automatically going to happen."

It was also known through Magic radio intercepts that a large proportion of Japanese military strength—land, sea, and air—was concentrating in the Indochina and South China Sea areas. No evidence of aircraft carriers had been found, however, either in those areas or in the Japanese mandated islands. Intelligence agencies, monitoring Japanese radio traffic, considered it probable that the carriers were still in their home waters, but they were not certain.

On this basis Marshall, Stark, and their respective staffs concluded that the Japanese were preparing to strike in Southeast Asia; this threat, of course, included the Philippine Commonwealth. Accordingly our Army and Navy commanders in the Philippines and at Guam had been specifically warned. The commanders in Hawaii, Panama, Alaska, and on the West Coast were kept informed of important developments.

This was the situation as Marshall and Stark saw it early on November 25. From that time on events succeeded one another with increasing rapidity, both in Washington and in Hawaii. This is how they unfolded:

Washington, Tuesday, November 25

Marshall and Stark attended a "War Council" meeting with the President, Secretary of State Cordell Hull, Secretary of War Henry L. Stimson, and Secretary of the Navy Frank Knox. Were the Japanese bluffing? Hull thought not; rejection of their terms would mean war. "These fellows mean to fight," he told the group. "You [Marshall and Stark] will have to be prepared."

Adequate preparation could not be guaranteed by either service chief. The great draft army was still only a partly disciplined mass. The Navy, better prepared for an immediate fight, was still far from ready for an extended period of combat. Marshall urged diplomatic delay. If the State Department could hold war off for even three months, the time gained would be precious, especially in the Philippines, where Douglas MacArthur's newly raised Commonwealth Army was only partly organized and equipped.

Perhaps the State Department's formula—*modus vivendi* they called it—which had been sent by cable to our British, Chinese, Australian, and Dutch allies for comment—would gain the needed time. This was a proposal for a three-month truce in Sino-Japanese hostilities, during which the United States, in return for Japan's withdrawal from southern Indochina, would make limited economic concessions to her.

It was evident to all concerned that otherwise hostilities were almost certain to break out within a few days. The President, noting Japan's proclivity for attacking without a declaration of war, impressed on all concerned that if war came, it must result from an initial blow by Japan. How, then, asked Roosevelt, could the United States permit this without too much danger to itself? *

That evening Stark wrote a lengthy warning to Kimmel in Hawaii, informing him that neither the President nor the Secretary of State "would be surprised over a Japanese surprise attack," adding that while "an attack upon the Philippines would be the most embarrassing thing that could happen to us . . . I still rather look for an advance into Thailand, Indochina, Burma Road areas as the most likely." Marshall re-

viewed the incoming and outgoing messages to overseas commanders, and busied himself with the almost numberless duties of his most important task: preparing our Army for combat.

Honolulu, Tuesday, November 25

Kimmel and Short had more than a passing interest in the status of our negotiations with Japan. Admiral Kimmel had been kept informed of the increasingly strained relations by frequent frank and newsy letters from Admiral Stark. One of these, dated November 7, had said in part: "Things seem to be moving steadily towards a crisis in the Pacific. . . . A month may see, literally, most anything . . . It doesn't look good."

Admiral Kimmel undoubtedly was thinking of that letter when he reread the official radio message which he had received the day before, November 24:

Chances of favorable outcomes of negotiations with Japan very doubtful . . . A surprise aggressive movement in any direction including attack on Philippines or Guam is a possibility. Chief of Staff has seen this dispatch, concurs and requests action addressees to inform senior Army officers their areas. Utmost secrecy necessary in order not to complicate an already tense situation or precipitate Japanese action.

Admiral Kimmel promptly sent a copy of the message to General Short. He had standing instructions to show such messages to the Army commander: the most critical messages from Washington were usually sent over Navy channels because the Army code was considered to be less secure. The Admiral saw no need for further action. After receiving a warning message on October 16 he had taken some measures for a partial alert and reported those promptly to Stark, who replied: "OK on the disposition which you made."

Admiral Kimmel and General Short had a cordial personal relationship, despite subsequent widespread but unfounded allegations to the contrary. They had frequently discussed, officially and personally, the possibility of a surprise Japanese attack and the measures to be taken to prepare for it and to thwart it if it should come. These plans had been approved in Washington. The Navy was responsible for long-range re-

---

* The claim has been advanced—notably by Rear Admiral Robert A. Theobald in *The Final Secret of Pearl Harbor* (Devin-Adair, 1954)—that President Roosevelt abetted the Japanese surprise "by causing the Hawaiian Commanders to be denied invaluable information from decoded Japanese dispatches concerning the rapid approach of the war and the strong probability that the attack would be directed at Pearl Harbor." He did so, according to now-retired Admiral Kimmel in a recent interview with United Press International, to "induce the Japanese to attack Pearl Harbor and thus permit him to honor his secret commitments to Great Britain and the Netherlands with the full support of the American people."

The report of the Army Pearl Harbor Board, submitted to the Secretary of War on October 20, 1944, apportioned a share of the blame for the surprise to the War and Navy Departments and

their top military officers in Washington. Even so, the service inquiries concluded that General Short and Admiral Kimmel had sufficient information to realize that war was imminent and had no excuse for inadequate security measures. They were not court-martialed, despite their requests, largely for political reasons. In this they were grievously wronged, for they had a right to be heard in their own defense. On the other hand, although I am not an apologist for the late President Roosevelt, it is simply ridiculous to suggest that he, who loved the Navy perhaps more than did any of our Presidents, would deliberately offer the Pacific Fleet as a sacrifice to entice Japan into war, and that this scheme was abetted by other responsible military men and statesmen. So many people would have known of such a nefarious plot that it would in fact have been impossible to muffle it.—T.N.D.

connaissance up to 700 miles, while the Army, with its land-based aircraft, was responsible for inshore reconnaissance for a distance up to twenty miles from shore. The Army's new radar would provide additional reconnaissance and air-warning service for a distance of up to 130 miles from Oahu. Periodically the commanders held joint maneuvers to test the plans and the readiness of their forces to carry them out.

They commanded large forces which might soon be called upon to fight, and it was essential that they maintain an intensive training schedule to assure the highest possible standard of combat efficiency. This was a formidable task, since many of their officers and men were inexperienced and untrained, having only recently been brought into our rapidly expanding armed forces. At the same time, as outpost commanders, both Short and Kimmel were well aware of their responsibilities for assuring the security of the fleet and of the island of Oahu.

Moreover, each commander assumed the other knew his business; each assumed the other's command was running on a full-time status. Each felt—as shown by later testimony—that to probe into the other's shop would be an unpardonable and resented intrusion. As a result, the liaison essential to any sort of joint or concerted operation—the daily constant and intimate exchange of details of command operations between Army and Navy staffs—was almost nonexistent. Each commander, then, was working in a partial vacuum.

On the single island of Oahu were concentrated most of the 42,857 troops that comprised the units of General Short's department. Carrying out the intensive training schedule was the bulk of two infantry divisions, less one regiment scattered in detachments on the other islands of the group. Also on Oahu were most of the antiaircraft and coast defense units of the Coast Artillery Command, and more than 250 aircraft of the Army's Hawaiian air force. Some of these aircraft, aloft on routine training exercises, were being tracked by the inexperienced crews of six Army mobile radar units newly installed at different points on the island.

There was comparable activity at the great Pearl Harbor Navy Yard, on the southern coast of the island, close by the bustling metropolis of Honolulu. Quite a few vessels of the U.S. Pacific Fleet were in port. Here Kimmel, the fleet's commander in chief, had his headquarters, from which he and his staff closely supervised the intense training programs of their ships in Hawaiian waters. The fleet comprised eight battleships, two aircraft carriers (with a total of 180 planes), sixteen cruisers, forty-five destroyers, twelve submarines, and slightly more than 300 land-based aircraft. In addition another battleship, an aircraft carrier, four cruisers, and various smaller vessels were temporarily absent, many being in mainland yards for repairs.

The Navy Yard itself was the principal installation of the Fourteenth Naval District; both base and the district were commanded by Rear Admiral Claude C. Bloch, who was a direct subordinate of Kimmel both as base commander and as a Pacific Fleet staff officer—a setup which bred no little confusion and which was not helped by the fact that Bloch was Kimmel's senior in the service, though not in command. Kimmel properly held Bloch responsible for the functioning and local security of all the land-based installations of the fleet in Hawaii, while he himself devoted his principal attention to the readiness of the fleet to function offensively at sea. He considered Bloch to be Short's naval counterpart, so far as local protection of the fleet in Hawaii was concerned. Formal co-ordination of Army and Navy activities in Hawaii and nearby Pacific areas, however, was done at conferences—fairly frequent—between Kimmel and Short.

[*On November 25 (Washington date line), Vice Admiral Chuichi Nagumo's First Air Fleet—six aircraft carriers and 414 combat planes, escorted by two battleships, two heavy cruisers and one light, and nine destroyers—put to sea from Tankan Bay in the southern Kurile Islands. Eight tank ships trailed it. Screening the advance were twenty-eight submarines which had left Kure a few days earlier.*

This powerful naval striking force had long been preparing for a surprise attack on the United States Pacific Fleet at Pearl Harbor. It did not, however, have a final directive to carry it out. The First Air Fleet was to leave the Kurile Islands and steam slowly east into the North Pacific to await orders either to attack or, if negotiations with the United States reached a conclusion satisfactory to Japan, to return home.]

Washington, Wednesday, November 26

Before attending a meeting of the Army-Navy Joint Board, both General Marshall and Admiral Stark had learned that Secretary of State Hull, with the full approval of the President, had made a momentous decision.

During the evening of the twenty-fifth and the early hours of the twenty-sixth, the State Department received the comments of our allies on the *modus vivendi* reply to the Japanese ultimatum. The British, Australians, and Dutch gave lukewarm approval to the proposal for a three-month truce, though in a personal message to the President, Prime Minister Winston Churchill remarked pointedly, "What about Chiang Kai-shek? Is he not having a very thin diet?"

Chiang, in fact, had protested violently against the truce proposal, which, with its relaxation of economic pressure on Japan, could only work to the psychological and military disadvantage of China. The protest, as well as information gleaned from more intercepted messages indicating that the Japanese would accept nothing less than complete agreement to their demands of November 20, caused Secretary Hull to doubt the wisdom of the *modus vivendi*. Obviously, these concessions were inadequate to satisfy Japanese demands, yet, because they would seem like American appeasement they would strike a major blow to Chinese morale.

Hull therefore recommended a different reply,

November 26, 1941: Kurusu and Nomura receive Hull's firm reply to their demands, and Japan's resolve grows stronger.

which the President approved. After a calm but firm restatement of the principles which had guided the American negotiations, the new note proposed, in essence: withdrawal of Japanese military forces from China and Indochina, recognition of the territorial integrity of those countries, unqualified acceptance of the National Government of China, and, finally, negotiation of a liberal U.S.-Japanese trade treaty once the other conditions had been met.

At 5 P.M. on November 26 Secretary Hull met with the two Japanese ambassadors and presented this reply

to them. Special envoy Kurusu read the note, then commented that his government would "throw up its hands" and that the American position practically "put an end to the negotiations."

By frequent phone calls, Secretary Hull had kept both Stimson and Knox informed of these rapid developments, and the two service secretaries had passed on the information to their senior military subordinates. So it was that when they met at a Joint Board conference that same day, Marshall and Stark were well aware of the course of the events still in progress at the State Department. Agreeing that war was now almost certain, they both felt that it was incumbent upon them to remind the President once more of the dangerous weakness of the Army and the Navy and particularly the grave danger of disaster in the Philippines if war were to break out before further reinforcements of men and matériel could reach General MacArthur. They directed their subordinates to have ready for their signatures the next day a joint memorandum to the President which would urge avoidance of hostilities for as long as possible consistent with national policy and national honor.

Late in the afternoon General Marshall held a conference with Major General Leonard T. Gerow, Chief of the War Plans Division, to discuss what should be done the next day, November 27. Marshall had planned to be in North Carolina that day to observe the final phases of the largest maneuvers in the Army's peacetime history; he felt he should carry out that intention, despite his concern about a report that a large Japanese troop convoy had moved into the South China Sea. The two officers discussed the grave implications of the growing Japanese concentrations in the Southeast Asia region. Even though he intended to be back at his desk on the twenty-eighth, General Marshall authorized Gerow to send overseas commanders a warning in his name if further information next day—the twenty-seventh—should point to the possibility of a surprise Japanese attack.

Honolulu, Wednesday, November 26

Admiral Kimmel received a report from the radio intelligence unit in Hawaii of a strong concentration of Japanese submarines and carrier aircraft in the Marshall Islands. This implied, but did not definitely prove, that some Japanese carriers were there as well. This information was perhaps inconsistent with a somewhat more definite report from the Philippines saying that radio traffic indicated all known Japanese carriers to be in home waters. Neither Admiral Kimmel nor members of his staff saw any need to inform General Short of these reports.

Short, meanwhile, had received an official message

Lieutenant General Walter C. Short

directing him to send two long-range B-24 bombers—due from the mainland—to photograph and observe the Japanese bases of Truk in the Caroline Islands and Jaluit in the Marshalls, reporting the number and locations of all Japanese naval vessels. He was to make sure both planes were "fully equipped with gun ammunition." But neither mission was ever flown: only one B-24 reached Short, and it was not properly equipped.

[*On the high seas, their bleak rendezvous at Tankan far astern, Nagumo's task force was steaming eastward. Radio silence was absolute. High-grade fuel kept smoke to a minimum. No waste was thrown overboard to leave telltale tracks; blackout on board was complete. Only the Admiral and a handful of his staff knew their orders; the rest of the command buzzed with speculation like so many hornets.*]

Washington, Thursday, November 27

General Gerow, summoned to Mr. Stimson's office, found Secretary Knox and Admiral Stark already there. The Secretary of War felt the time had come to alert General MacArthur in the Philippines. He told his listeners that Secretary Hull had warned him no peaceful solution was apparent. "I have washed my hands of it," Hull had said, "and it is now in the hands of you and Knox, the Army and the Navy."

Stimson added word of a telephone discussion with the President, who, agreeing that an alert order be sent out, desired all commanders to be cautioned that Japan must commit the first overt act of war. All four in Stimson's office then prepared drafts of alert messages to be sent to General MacArthur and Admiral Hart in the Philippines and to Army and Navy commanders in Hawaii, Panama, and on the West Coast.

Early in the afternoon Gerow sent out the warning:

Negotiations with Japan appear to be terminated to all practicable purposes with only the barest possibilities that the Japanese Government might . . . offer to continue.

The message then reiterated Mr. Roosevelt's desire that Japan commit the first overt act. But this, it was pointed out,

should not repeat not be construed as restricting you to a course . . . that might jeopardize your defense. *Prior to hostile Japanese action you are directed to undertake such reconnaissance and other measures as you deem necessary* [italics supplied], but these measures should be carried out so as not repeat not to alarm civil population or disclose intent. Report measures taken . . .

The message further directed that, should hostilities occur, commanders would undertake offensive tasks in accordance with existing war plans. It concluded with the caution that dissemination of "this highly secret information" should be limited to the essential minimum.

Stark's message to Navy commanders (as well as to our special naval observer in London, who was to advise the British) was sent at the same time; it opened bluntly: "This dispatch is to be considered a war warning." It related the end of negotiations and the expectation that "an aggressive move" might come within the next few days. Then, in contrast to the more general Army warning, it added the information that known military activities of the Japanese indicated they probably intended to launch "an amphibious expedition against either the Philippines, Thai or Kra peninsula or possibly Borneo." Like the Army warning, it directed execution of existing war plans in the event of hostilities. Naval commanders in the continental United States, Guam, and Samoa were cautioned to take antisabotage measures.

If read together, these two messages definitely pointed a finger at Southeast Asia as the expected enemy target. This, of course, in no way excuses any of the subsequent actions of our commanders in Hawaii, whose paramount responsibility was the security of their post. But it must have influenced their thinking.

Honolulu, Thursday, November 27

The official warnings from Washington confirmed to Short and Kimmel the seriousness of the international situation. Short, who noted that he was expected to report the measures he was taking, sent the following reply: "Report Department alerted to prevent sabotage. Liaison with the Navy."

The Hawaiian Department plans provided for three kinds of alert. Number 1, which was what Short had ordered, was to guard against sabotage and uprisings—long a preoccupation of all Hawaiian commanders because of the high proportion of Japanese in the Islands. Number 2 included security against possible isolated, external air or naval attacks. Number 3 was a full-scale deployment for maximum defense of the

Islands, and particularly of Oahu—heart of the military organization. Only in the two higher stages of alert was ammunition to be distributed to the anti-aircraft batteries; in Alert No. 1 all ammunition was to be kept stored in the dumps. Under Alert No. 1, planes would be parked closely for easy guarding; under the others they would be dispersed.

General Short felt he was confirmed in his concern over sabotage when his intelligence officer—or G-2—presented a message from the War Department G-2, warning that "subversive activities may be expected."

In obedience to the instruction to make such reconnaissance as he might "deem necessary," Short did, however, order his newly installed radar stations to operate daily from 4 A.M. to 7 A.M.; these were the dawn hours when surprise attack was most likely. Further reconnaissance, he felt, was the Navy's responsibility. He didn't know that Kimmel was having troubles of his own in attempting any sustained offshore reconnaissance. Nor was Kimmel aware that Short's radar was operating only on a curtailed basis.

Kimmel pondered over what steps he should take. Though he was already alerted to some extent, he knew that for the moment he could do little in the way of "defensive deployment" in his war plan tasks—most specifically, raids into the Japanese mandated islands. Should he then prepare for an attack against Oahu? The Washington message implied that this was not a probability. Even so, he didn't have sufficient planes for a 360 degree, distant reconnaissance from Oahu.

In compliance with instructions from Washington, Kimmel was sending some Marine planes to Wake and Midway islands. He decided that the two carrier task forces he was ordering to carry out this instruction could, en route, conduct long-range searches to the west, over the direct route from Japan to Oahu.

Task Force 8, under Vice Admiral William F. Halsey, including the carrier *Enterprise* and three cruisers, was leaving that day. In conference with Halsey before departure, Kimmel showed him the "war warning" message. Halsey asked how far he should go if he met any Japanese ships while searching. "Use your common sense," was Kimmel's reply. Halsey, it is understood, commented that these were the best orders he could receive, adding that if he found as much as one Japanese sampan, he would sink it. Kimmel, by making no further comment, apparently acquiesced.

Pending the arrival of Halsey at Wake, Kimmel sent orders to a patrol plane squadron based on Midway to proceed to Wake and return, searching ocean areas and covering a 525-mile area around Wake itself.

Kimmel felt that he had done all he could in that line without completely halting fleet training and ex-

hausting the pilots of his relatively weak air command. But he did order immediate attack on any and all unidentified submarines discovered in the vicinity of Oahu and other fleet operating zones. Neither then nor later, apparently, did he check on the local security measures undertaken by Admiral Bloch's command, nor did he suggest any co-ordination between Bloch and Short.

[*Nagumo's force was steady on a course laid between the Aleutians and Midway Island, the carriers in two parallel rows of three each. Battleships and cruisers guarded the flanks, destroyers screened wide, and submarines were scouting far ahead.*]

Washington, Friday, November 28

General Marshall, back from his North Carolina inspection, was briefed by Gerow on the previous day's happenings. He read and approved the joint memorandum, already signed by Admiral Stark, which urged on the President the need for gaining time, particularly until troops—some already at sea and nearing Guam, others about to embark on the West Coast—could reach the Philippines. He also approved the warning message Gerow had sent to the overseas commanders.

At noon he attended the President's "War Council" meeting at the White House. The implications of a large Japanese amphibious force, known to be sailing southward through the South China Sea, were discussed. British Malaya, the Netherlands East Indies, and the Philippines were potential targets, the invasion of which would immediately involve us in war. But unless Congress should previously declare war, the United States could not attack this force. It was agreed that the President should send a message to Emperor Hirohito urging him to preserve peace, and that Mr. Roosevelt should also address Congress, explaining the dangers being created by this Japanese aggressive action. The President then left for a short vacation at

Rear Admiral Husband E. Kimmel

Warm Springs, Georgia, directing his advisers to have the two documents prepared in his absence.

Marshall, back at his desk, thumbed through a sheaf of radio replies to the "war warning" message. Lieutenant General John L. DeWitt, commanding on the Pacific Coast, reported instituting a harbor alert at San Francisco and similar precautions in Alaska in liaison with naval authorities. He requested permission to direct air as well as ground deployment of his far-flung command. It was a long message, contrasting sharply with Short's succinct report of sabotage defense measures in Hawaii. But the Chief of Staff didn't pay much attention; it would be Gerow's job to handle any necessary responses. So Marshall initialed most of the messages and then forgot about them.

Short's message, however, was not initialed by Marshall. He would later testify he had no recollection of ever having seen it, although it bore the routine rubber stamp, "Noted by Chief of Staff."

As for Admiral Stark, he was pushing off a long message to Navy commanders on the West Coast, and to Admiral Kimmel, quoting the Army alert message of the twenty-seventh, including its admonition that Japan must commit the first "overt act."

Honolulu, Friday, November 28

Kimmel read Stark's long quote of the Army's alert message. He was particularly interested in its stress that "if hostilities cannot . . . be avoided the United States desires that Japan commit the first overt act." This appeared to confirm his decision of the previous day: limiting defensive deployment to one patrol squadron cruising from Wake to Midway and sending carrier task forces for local defense of those outposts.

Admiral Kimmel received several other interesting reports. The U.S.S. *Helena* reported contact with an unidentified submarine. An intelligence estimate based on radio intercepts indicated Japanese carriers were still in their own home waters. Another report on intercepted Japanese messages established a "winds code," by means of which Japan would notify its diplomatic and consular representatives abroad of a decision to go to war: "east wind rain" meant war with the United States; "north wind cloudy," war with Russia; "west wind clear," war with England and invasion of Thailand, Malaya, and the Dutch East Indies.

It was all very interesting. However, the Admiral never thought of mentioning any of these reports during his conference with General Short that day. They discussed mutual responsibility for security of Wake and Midway—in light of the mixed Army-Navy garrisons at both places. But neither thought of asking the other what action he had taken on the November 27 warnings, nor did either volunteer any information on matters he considered to be of interest to his own individual service only.

[*Admiral Nagumo's fleet spent the day in attempts to refuel in a plunging sea—an operation which, as it turned out, would continue for several days under almost heartbreaking conditions of bad weather.*]

Washington, Saturday, November 29

Both General Marshall and Admiral Stark received Magic copies of more intercepted Japanese messages. One of these from Premier Tojo in Tokyo to the ambassadors in Washington was quite ominous:

The United States' . . . humiliating proposal . . . was quite unexpected and extremely regrettable. The Imperial Government can by no means use it as a basis for negotiations. Therefore . . . in two or three days the negotiations will be de facto ruptured. . . . However, I did not wish you to give the impression that the negotiations are broken off. Merely say to them that you are awaiting instructions. . . . From now on, do the best you can.

To Marshall and Stark this was clear evidence indeed that the Japanese were stalling for time only long enough to get their forces ready to attack in the Indonesia-Southeast Asia area. It seemed now only a question of time, as more reports streamed in about Japanese convoys moving into the South China Sea.

For a good part of the morning Stark and Marshall were working closely with Secretaries Knox and Stimson in preparing and revising drafts of the presidential messages to Congress and to Emperor Hirohito, in accordance with the agreement at the previous day's meeting of the War Council. Finally, about noon, the two secretaries were satisfied, and their proposed drafts were sent to Secretary Hull.

Late in the afternoon both read with considerable interest reports of a warlike speech which Premier Tojo had delivered that day (November 30, Tokyo time). The twenty-ninth had been the deadline established in the messages from Tokyo to the ambassadors. The speech, while violently warlike in tone, failed to give any indication of Japanese intentions.

Honolulu, Saturday, November 29

Things were generally quiet on Oahu and in the outlying waters, as the Army and Navy both began a weekend of relaxation after five days of strenuous training. There was considerable bustle, however, at the Army's headquarters at Fort Shafter, as well as at Navy headquarters at nearby Pearl Harbor. General Short approved a message in reply to the latest sabotage warning from Washington, outlining in detail the security measures which had been taken. Admiral Kimmel received another message from Washington reminding him once more that he was to be prepared to carry out existing war plans in the event of hostilities with Japan. Thus, once again, the two commanders were reminded of the alert messages they had received on the twenty-seventh, and once again they found themselves satisfied with the actions they had then taken.

[*In the North Pacific Admiral Nagumo's fleet continued refueling.*]

Washington, Sunday, November 30

General Marshall, returning from his usual Sunday morning horseback ride at Fort Myer, found another intercepted Japanese message awaiting him; the Foreign Ministry was cautioning its envoys in Washington to keep talking and "be careful that this does not lead to anything like a breaking-off of negotiations." He agreed with G-2's conclusion that the Japanese were stalling until their South China Sea assault was ready.

Stark, at his desk, was called that morning by Secretary of State Hull, gravely concerned about Premier Tojo's warlike speech. The Secretary told him he was going to urge the President's return from Warm Springs. A later call from Hull informed Stark that President Roosevelt would be back Monday morning; Stark must see the President and report on the naval developments in the Far East.

Honolulu, Sunday, November 30

General Short, in light of his instructions "not to alarm the civil population," must have been annoyed to read the Honolulu *Advertiser* headlines that morning: "Hawaii Troops Alerted." There wasn't anything he could do about it, however; even the limited nature of his Alert No. 1 would draw newspaper attention in a critical time such as this. He also read that "Leaders Call Troops Back in Singapore—Hope Wanes as Nations Fail at Parleys" and "Kurusu Bluntly Warned Nation Ready for Battle."

Kimmel ordered a squadron of patrol planes to Midway, to replace temporarily the squadron which he had ordered to reconnoiter about Wake. He was also interested in an information copy of a Navy Department message to Admiral Hart, commanding our Asiatic Fleet at Manila, directing him to scout for information as to an intended Japanese attack on the Kra Isthmus of Thailand, just north of Malaya.

Kimmel didn't think that war could be delayed much longer. He wrote on the top of a piece of paper the words—"Steps to be taken in case of American-Japanese war within the next twenty-four hours," an *aide-mémoire* of the orders he must issue to his fleet.

[*The Japanese First Air Fleet was still engaged in the arduous refueling job, while continuing its eastward course at slow speed.*]

Washington, Monday, December 1

A busy day. Stark learned from his intelligence staff that the Japanese Navy had changed service radio frequencies and call letters for all units afloat—a normal prewar step. He went to the White House with Secretary Hull and briefed the President.

In the afternoon both Stark and Marshall digested an unusual number of important Magic intercepts of Japanese messages. Japan's Foreign Minister was urging his ambassadors to prevent the United States "from becoming unduly suspicious," emphasizing that it was important to give the impression to the Americans that "negotiations are continuing." Tokyo also had ordered its diplomatic offices in London, Hong Kong, Singapore, and Manila "to abandon the use of code machines and to dispose of them." Japan's ambassador at Bangkok reported his intrigues to maneuver Thailand into a declaration of war on Great Britain.

But most significant was an exchange between Japan's ambassador to Berlin and his foreign office. The ambassador reported that Foreign Minister von Ribbentrop had given him Hitler's unequivocal assurance that "should Japan become engaged in a war against the United States, Germany, of course, would join the war immediately." Tojo promptly told the ambassador to inform the German government that "war may suddenly break out between the Anglo-Saxon nations and Japan through some clash of arms. . . . This war may come quicker than anyone dreams."

And how quickly would that be? This was the question which sprang immediately to the minds of Admiral Stark and General Marshall, the men responsible for readying the armed forces of the United States for the coming clash of arms. They had no way of knowing that the answer lay in a brief uncoded message picked up by several American radio intelligence intercept stations just a few hours earlier. "Climb Mount Niitaka," was the message. No significance could be attached to it, so it never came to the attention of Marshall or Stark. Nor would it have meant anything to either of them.

Honolulu, Monday, December 1

Kimmel and Short held another routine conference. Presumably they discussed at some length the grave international situation. Supplementing the cryptic but alarming official intelligence reports and warnings were the headlines blazoning the Honolulu newspapers.

But neither Kimmel nor Short in their conversation discussed local security precautions or a possible threat to Oahu. Politely but inconclusively they continued discussion of the divided responsibility at Wake and Midway. Kimmel never thought to mention to Short that he had received another Washington warning about the "winds code" and that he had also been informed of the change in Japanese military frequencies and call letters. It never occurred to Kimmel that Short might not have been told about either matter.

Routine training continued in Army posts. General Short was quite pleased that his limited alert—which the War Department had apparently approved—had not interfered noticeably with training programs.

[*"Climb Mount Niitaka!"*

Admiral Nagumo sucked in his breath as the message was laid before him this day. This was it; the pre-arranged code which meant "Proceed with attack."

Obedient to the signal flags broken out aboard the flagship, the gray ships came foaming about to a south-easterly course, vibrating to the thrust of increased propeller speed. Inside the steel hulls the mustered crews, learning the news, cheered, quaffed sake, and burned incense to the spirits of their ancestors.]

Washington, Tuesday, December 2

Additional Magic intercepts indicated further Japanese preparations for war, with the enemy's known offensive weight still massing in Southeast Asia.

Honolulu, Tuesday, December 2

Kimmel, discussing intelligence reports with his staff, noted the change in Japanese radio frequencies as related in the Navy Department's fortnightly intelligence summary, received late the previous day. The gist of it was that Tokyo was preparing for "operations on a large scale."

Then Kimmel called for intelligence estimates on the location of Japanese aircraft carriers. Captain Edwin T. Layton, his intelligence officer, gave estimated locations for all except Divisions 1 and 2—four carriers.

"What!" exclaimed Kimmel, "you don't know where [they] are?"

"No, sir, I do not. I think they are in home waters, but—"

Sternly, but with a suspicion of a twinkle in his eyes, Kimmel delivered himself of a masterpiece of unconscious irony.

BILLY MITCHELL'S PROPHECY

In the fall of 1923, Brigadier General William "Billy" Mitchell, then Assistant Chief of the young Army Air Service, was sent on an inspection tour of the Pacific. Upon his return, Mitchell publicly voiced opinions about the inadequacies of our Pacific defenses and the very real threat of Japanese aggression that caused a furor in the War Department.

Among other things Mitchell warned that the Hawaiian Islands—and, in particular, the great naval base at Pearl Harbor—were open to a Japanese surprise air attack. He then proceeded to outline how such an attack could be made successfully. Because Mitchell failed to reckon on the development of the aircraft carrier, many details of his plan now seem unnecessarily elaborate, if not fantastic; but in the light of what happened on December 7, 1941, his total concept proved alarmingly accurate.

The prophetic words which appear below are published for the first time. They are taken from the original report that Mitchell wrote in 1924—a 525-page manuscript recently brought to light after years of obscurity in the classified files of the War Department and the National Archives.—Ed.

I. The Military Importance of the Island of Oahu
1. Assuming a state of war to be impending and with the mission of the Hawaiian Department to be the holding of the Island of Oahu for four months before the arrival of supporting troops, let us estimate what the action of Japan will be. . . . She knows full well that the United States will probably enter the next war with the methods and weapons of the former war, and will, therefore, offer the enticing morsel which all nations that have followed this system have done before. Japan also knows full well that the defense of the Hawaiian Group is based on the defense of the Island of Oahu and not on the defense of the whole group.
2. The Island of Oahu, with its military depots, both naval and land, its airdromes, water supplies, the city of Honolulu with its wharves and supply points, forms an easy, compact and convenient object for air attack. . . .

II. Possible Plan of Attack of the Hawaiian Islands and Results Thereof.
1. There is no adequate defense against air attack except an air force. This can be supplemented by auxiliaries on the ground, such as cannon, machine guns, and balloon barrages, but without air power these arrangements act only to give a false sense of security, such as the ostrich must feel when he hides his head in the sand. . . .
2. I believe, therefore, that should Japan decide upon the reduction and seizure of the Hawaiian Islands, the following procedure would be adopted. Ten submarines would be loaded with six pursuit airplanes and spares each, the airplane crates being made in two segments so that each one

could be used as a barge when emptied of its cargo. These crates would be carried as deck loads, the boats would dive only for concealment. Two airplane transports would be provided, each loaded with fifty bombardment planes. These ships could be equipped with a flying-off deck laid down in sections while the transports were in use. These seacraft would be started so as to arrive at the islands of Niihau [the smallest and westernmost of the Hawaiian Islands, it is now privately owned and operated as a sheep ranch—Ed.] and Midway respectively on "D" day.

3. The submarines with the pursuit equipment aboard would land at Niihau on the evening of "D" day and, as there are only 140 people on the island, no radio station or other means of communication, except by water, probably the first information of this force, received at Honolulu, would be the appearance of the hostile aircraft. . . .

4. The pursuit ships could be set up and made ready for service during the night and be ready for duty the next morning. (Twenty submarines could carry twice as many pursuit ships as the ten mentioned above.) The force destined for Midway Island could debark its bombardment equipment from the transports, prepare the airdrome in the sand with landing mats and the necessary auxiliaries to the aircraft. All the islands between Midway and Niihau would be occupied with observation posts and radio sets.

5. The flying time between Midway to Niihau is eleven hours. By equipping the bombers with auxiliary gas tanks in their bomb compartments a cruising ability of about sixteen hours can easily be given them. As soon as set up and tested, those ships would fly to Niihau and be ready to attack Oahu immediately afterwards. While these operations are taking place the Island of Guam would be seized. (Under these conditions the Philippines would fall of their own weight within a year or two.)

6. The distance from Niihau to Honolulu is about 150 miles, or an hour and a half flight, or a total of three hours there and back; allowing forty minutes for an attack and an additional twenty minutes for eventualities would require a maximum of four hours for one attack mission. (The present United States pursuit airplane with auxiliary gas tank has four and a half hours' fuel; the bomber, about six.)

7. The first attack would be arranged as follows: Japanese pursuit, sixty ships, organized into one group of three squadrons of twenty ships each; two squadrons to participate in combined attack with bombardment and one squadron to remain in reserve on the alert. . . . The objectives for attack are: (1) Ford Island airdrome hangars, storehouses, and ammunition dumps (2) Navy fuel oil tanks (3) Water supply of Honolulu (4) Water supply of Schofield (5) Schofield Barracks airdrome and troop establishments (6) Naval submarine station (7) City and wharves of Honolulu

8. Attack will be launched as follows:

Bombardment

Attack to be made on Ford's Island at 7:30 A.M. . . .

"Do you mean to say they could be rounding Diamond Head and you wouldn't know it?"

The conference ended after a discussion on the difficulty of locating a force operating under sealed orders while preserving radio silence.

Short met Kimmel that day again. They continued debate over jurisdiction at Wake and Midway.

[*Nagumo's fleet was steadily driving south toward Oahu. In prearranged code—unintelligible to American Magic interceptors—Tokyo had confirmed the target date: "X-Day will be 8 December"—December 7, Honolulu time.*]

Washington, Wednesday, December 3

Along with the other recipients of Magic information, General Marshall and Admiral Stark noted but attached no particular significance to a pair of intercepted messages made available to them that day.

One, dated November 15, was already old; its translation had been deferred for several days in order to take care of messages considered more urgent. It referred to an earlier message directing the Japanese consulate at Honolulu to make periodic reports on the location of American warships in Pearl Harbor, and requested the Honolulu consulate to step up these reports to twice a week.

No particular importance was attributed to this by Admiral Stark or his senior naval intelligence officers, since the Japanese had long been making efforts to obtain information about the activities and number of ships in harbor at other naval bases on the West Coast and at Panama. The fact that the Japanese wanted more complete data, including exact locations of specific vessels in Pearl Harbor, was assumed to be merely an indication of their thoroughness in evaluating intelligence on America's main Pacific combat force.

The other message was a reply by Prime Minister Tojo to the suggestion of his ambassadors at Washington that peace could perhaps be preserved through a high-level conference—they had proposed former Premier Prince Konoye as the Japanese envoy and Vice President Henry Wallace or Presidential Assistant Harry Hopkins for the United States—at "some midway point, such as Honolulu." Tojo's response, that "it would be inappropriate for us to propose such a meeting," seemed a less significant indication of Japan's immediate intentions than the continuing reports of her movements in and near Indochina.

Honolulu, Wednesday, December 3

Admiral Kimmel noted the continuing and surprising lack of information on Japanese carriers contained in the latest daily radio intelligence summary, which stated that "carrier traffic is at a low ebb."

That day, too, he received Admiral Stark's letter of November 25. He agreed with Stark's view that "an attack on the Philippines" might be embarrassing, but that "an advance into Thailand, Indochina, Burma Road area [was] most likely."

In the afternoon Short and Kimmel conferred. They soon got into a grim discussion of what they could do to carry out assigned war plans when and if war broke out. Both were thinking, of course, of planned naval and air raids into the Marshall Islands and of security measures for Wake and Midway. There was no mention of like measures for Oahu. Nor did Admiral Kimmel think to mention to General Short his latest intelligence reports about the burning of Japanese codes or the missing aircraft carriers.

[Nagumo's planners on the high seas were busy marking on their charts of Pearl Harbor the exact locations of six of the U.S. battle fleet—the Pennsylvania, Arizona, California, Tennessee, Maryland, and West Virginia. The data came from Honolulu, relayed by radio through Imperial Navy Headquarters in Tokyo.]

Washington, Thursday, December 4

A mixed bag of Magic intercepts available to both Stark and Marshall gave clear indication of Japanese intentions to go to war. Instructions came to Ambassador Nomura to completely destroy one of the two special machines for secret coding, but to hold the other and its cipher key—which should be in his personal possession—"until the last minute." One intercepted message, considered to be relatively insignificant, was to the Japanese consul at Honolulu; he was to "investigate completely the fleet-bases in the neighborhood of the Hawaiian military reservation."

Stark and Marshall concerned themselves with routine activities.

Honolulu, Thursday, December 4

Admiral Kimmel conferred with two of his senior task-force commanders, scheduled to sail the next day on combined training-alert missions. One, under Vice Admiral Wilson Brown, was to proceed to Johnson Island, 700 miles southwest of Oahu, on a joint Navy-Marine bombardment and landing exercise. The other, under Rear Admiral T. H. Newton, included the carrier Lexington. This force was to go to Midway Island, fly off a squadron of Marine planes to reinforce the local garrison, and then rendezvous with Brown at Johnson Island. En route the Lexington's planes would conduct routine scouting flights.

Kimmel's intention was that, should war break out, these forces would be available for raids into the Marshall Island group in accordance with existing war plans. Both task-force commanders understood their

war-plan missions; both were aware in general of the tense international situation. Kimmel, therefore, felt he was under no obligation to inform either of Washington's November 27 "war warning" message.

The net naval situation on Oahu now was that the entire carrier force of the Pacific Fleet was either at sea or about to steam and that the approaches to the island from the west would be scouted for several days to come.

Kimmel felt that these steps would ensure a reconnaissance search of a large portion of the central Pacific Ocean, as extensive as his limited aircraft strength would permit. But, from the Hawaiian Islands north to the Aleutians, both sea and air were still bare of American reconnaissance.

Kimmel and Short did not meet that day.

[Admiral Nagumo, watching the intermittent refueling being carried on during the day, was intrigued to learn from Honolulu, via Tokyo, that watchful Japanese eyes were "unable to ascertain whether air alert had been issued. There are no indications of sea alert. . . ."]

Washington, Friday, December 5

Both War and Navy departments were busy compiling data for President Roosevelt on Japanese sea, land, and air strength concentrating in French Indochina and adjacent areas. In an intercepted Japanese message from Washington, Ambassador Nomura told Tokyo that in case of Japanese invasion of Thailand, joint military action by Great Britain and the United States "is a definite certainty, with or without a declaration of war." Another, from Tokyo, reiterated the previous instructions about destruction of codes and coding machines.

Admiral Stark, conferring with staff officers, decided no further warning orders need be sent to overseas naval commanders; the message of November 27 was adequate. All concurred.

Honolulu, Friday, December 5

General Short read with interest a cryptic message from G-2 in Washington to his intelligence officer, directing him to get in touch with the Navy immediately "regarding broadcasts from Tokyo reference weather." So Lieutenant Colonel George W. Bicknell, assistant G-2, gave the General all facts obtainable from his own office and from Kimmel's headquarters. Short was informed by Kimmel of the departure of the two naval task forces of Admirals Brown and Newton.

[While pilots and squadron leaders on board Nagumo's fleet studied and restudied their coming roles, the ships —900 miles north of Midway and 1,300 miles northwest of Oahu—slid slowly down the North Pacific rollers, *still far beyond the range of any American search plane.*]

Washington, Saturday, December 6

Reports of increasing Japanese concentration and movements in Indochina, South China, and the South China Sea absorbed Stark and Marshall, as well as all the other members of the War Cabinet from the President down. Mr. Roosevelt, the service chiefs were glad to learn, had decided that he would personally warn Emperor Hirohito that further aggressions might lead to war and urge the Japanese ruler that withdrawal of his forces from Indochina "would result in the assurance of peace throughout the whole of the South Pacific area."

Late in the afternoon Magic plucked out of the air thirteen parts of a fourteen-part memorandum from Tokyo to the Japanese envoys. This much of the message summarized negotiations from the Japanese viewpoint, concluding that the American note of November 26 was not "a basis of negotiations." The envoys were instructed to handle it carefully, since "the situation is extremely delicate."

Distribution of this intercept was curious. Decoding was completed after office hours. General Sherman A. Miles, Army G-2, saw no need to disturb either the Secretary of War, General Marshall, or General Gerow at their homes. (In passing it might be mentioned that one didn't disturb General Marshall at home without extremely good reason.) Some Navy people saw the message. Stark, who was at the theater, learned of it when he returned home and found that he was expected to call the White House. The President had received the intercept, as had the State Department. The details of the conversation are not known, but presumably the President told Stark, as he had earlier said to Harry Hopkins: "This means war!"

Honolulu, Saturday, December 6

In the daily radio intelligence summary received that morning from Washington, Admiral Kimmel was again struck by lack of information on the location of Japanese carriers. In other dispatches, however, there was considerable information about different kinds of Japanese activity. He received a copy of Admiral Hart's message reporting on the movement of the two convoys south of Indochina. And he received a message from Washington authorizing him, "in view of the international situation and the exposed position of our outlying Pacific Islands," to order the destruction of classified documents at these islands, "now or under

later conditions of greater emergency." Neither the Admiral nor any member of his staff saw any need to pass on any information to the Army. Presumably General Short was getting it all through Army channels.

Carefully checking the reported locations of all fleet units and projecting their planned routes for the next twenty-four hours, Admiral Kimmel again made his daily revision of his personal check-list memorandum: "Steps to be taken in case of American-Japanese war within the next twenty-four hours."

Over at Fort Shafter, Army headquarters, the daily staff conference was as usual presided over by Colonel Walter C. Phillips, chief of staff. General Short did not normally attend these meetings. Bicknell, assistant G-2, who seems to have been on his toes those days, reported the Japanese consulate in Honolulu was busily burning and destroying secret papers, significant in light of similar reports throughout the world already noted in the intercepts. The chief of staff and G-2 reported this information later to General Short.

And so Oahu drifted into another weekend: a time of relaxation for both Army and Navy. Short, however, was interrupted by Bicknell early that evening at his quarters while he and his G-2—Colonel Kendall Fielder —and their wives were about to drive to a dinner dance.

Bicknell, with some sense of urgency, reported that the local FBI agent had passed to him and to Navy intelligence a transcript of a suspicious long-distance telephone message. A Japanese named Mori, talking to someone in Tokyo, mentioned flights of airplanes, searchlights, and the number of ships in Pearl Harbor, along with cryptic reference to various flowers—apparently part of some sort of code.

Both the FBI man and Bicknell were alarmed at the implications of this flower code. Neither Short nor

Opana station, northern Oahu, 7 A.M.: The Army radar watch closes down, but Private Lockard keeps his mobile set going. At 7:02, he starts tracking a strange formation of planes.

Fielder, however, was disturbed. Short, before they hurried to the car where their wives awaited them impatiently, told Bicknell he was, perhaps, "too intelligence-conscious." In any event they could talk about it again in the morning.

The district intelligence officer of the Navy decided that the transcript should be studied further by a Japanese linguist and so put the FBI report away until Monday morning. Admiral Kimmel was not informed.

[*Nagumo's fleet, the wallowing tankers now left behind, was churning southward at twenty-four-knot speed. By 6 A.M. next day it would be 230 miles north of Oahu with its planes thrusting skyward. And at dawn, five midget two-man submarines—disgorged from five large Japanese submarines gathered offshore that night—poked their way around Diamond Head, Pearl Harbor-bound.*]

Washington, Sunday, December 7

By 8 A.M. the last part of the Japanese memorandum—Part Fourteen—had been intercepted, transcribed, and was ready for distribution. Both Army and Navy intelligence officers were slightly surprised at its mild tone: "The Japanese Government regrets . . . that it is impossible to reach an agreement through further negotiations."

Stark got it in his office. Marshall was taking his Sunday morning recreational ride at Fort Myer: the message would await his arrival—usually at about 11 A.M. All others concerned got it. Meanwhile two other messages had been intercepted by Magic, and Colonel Rufus Bratton, executive officer in G-2, was so upset by them he tried vainly to get them to the Chief of Staff.

One of the messages ordered the embassy to destroy immediately its one remaining cipher machine plus all codes and secret documents. The other read:

"Will the Ambassador please submit to the United States Government (if possible to the Secretary of State) our reply to the United States at 1 P.M. on the 7th, your time."

It will be remembered that General Marshall did not take kindly to interruptions in his off-duty hours. So, despite the limited area of his ride—an automobile or motorcycle from Fort Myer headquarters could have intercepted him in fifteen minutes at most—not until his return to his quarters at ten-thirty did Marshall learn that an important message was awaiting him. He reached his office in the Munitions Building at about 11:15, to find General Gerow, General Miles, and Colonel Bratton there. Bratton handed him the three intercepted messages—the memorandum, the instructions to destroy codes and papers, and the instruction to deliver the Japanese answer at 1 P.M. precisely.

Marshall read quickly but carefully, as was usual with him. Then—

"Something is going to happen at one o'clock," he told the officers. "When they specified a day, that of course had significance, but not comparable to an hour."

He immediately called Stark, who had read all three messages. A warning should be sent at once to all Pacific commanders, Marshall felt. Stark hesitated; he felt all had already been alerted. Marshall stated that in view of the "one o'clock" item he would apprise Army commanders anyway.

Hanging up, he reached for a pencil and drafted his instruction to DeWitt, Western Defense Command; Andrews, Panama Command; Short, Hawaiian Command; and MacArthur, Philippine Command. It took him about three minutes. He read it to the group:

"The Japanese are presenting at 1 P.M. E.S.T. today, what amounts to an ultimatum. Also they are under orders to destroy their code machine immediately. Just what significance the hour set may have, we do not know, but be on alert accordingly."

As he was ordering Bratton to send it out at once, Stark telephoned back. Would Marshall please include in his dispatch the "usual expression to inform the naval officer?" Marshall quickly added the words "Inform naval authorities of this communication." He sent Bratton on his way, instructing him to return as soon as the message had been delivered to the message center.

Bratton was back in five minutes; he had delivered the message personally to the officer in charge of the message center, Colonel French.

Marshall, obviously more perturbed than any of those present had ever before seen him, asked Bratton how much time would be consumed in enciphering and dispatching the message. Bratton didn't know. So back he was rushed to find out.

Marshall, it developed, was pondering whether or not he should telephone a warning—especially to Mac-Arthur. Time was running out; not much more than one hour remained. Marshall had a "scrambler" phone on his desk, which permitted secure long-distance conversations with similar phones in the headquarters of overseas commanders; eavesdroppers would hear only unintelligible gibberish. Marshall, however, must have had some private reservations as to the efficacy of the scrambler mechanism, and apparently feared that the Japanese might have some way of deciphering the conversation. A telephone call which could not be kept secret might precipitate Japanese action; it would almost certainly indicate we had broken their secret code. Would it be worth it?

Bratton reported back that the process would take about thirty minutes.

"Thirty minutes until it is dispatched, or thirty minutes until it is received and decoded at the other end?"

Business of rushing back to the message center again, while the big office clock ticked away. Bratton, charging back, announced that the message, decoded, would be in the hands of the addressees in thirty minutes. It was now precisely noon. In Hawaii it was only 6:30 A.M. Marshall, satisfied, made no further follow-up.

Had he done so he would have found out that Colonel French at the message center was having some troubles. To San Francisco, Panama, and Manila the warning sped without delay. But the War Department radio, so Colonel French was informed, had been out of contact with Hawaii since 10:20 that morning. French decided to use commercial facilities: Western Union to San Francisco, thence commercial radio to Honolulu. This was a normal procedure; usually it would mean but little further delay. French never dreamed of disturbing the Chief of Staff by reporting such trivia. So Marshall's warning was filed at the Army Signal Center at 12:01 P.M. (6:31 A.M. in Ha-

waii); teletype transmission to San Francisco was completed by 12:17 P.M. (6:47 A.M. in Hawaii), and was in the Honolulu office of RCA at 1:03 P.M. Washington time (7:33 A.M. in Hawaii). Since that was too early for teletype traffic to Fort Shafter, RCA sent it by motorcycle messenger. He would, as it turned out, be delayed through extraordinary circumstances.

Honolulu, Sunday, December 7

Extraordinary circumstances had become almost commonplace on and near Oahu as early as 3:42 A.M. At that hour the mine sweeper *Condor*, conducting a routine sweep of the harbor entrance, sighted a submarine periscope. This was a defensive area where American submarines were prohibited from operating submerged. The *Condor* flashed a report of the sighting to the destroyer *Ward*, of the inshore patrol. For two hours the *Ward* searched the harbor entrance in vain; meanwhile the *Condor* and another mine sweeper had entered the harbor at about 5 A.M.; for some reason the antisubmarine net, opened to permit the entrance of the mine sweepers, was not closed.

At 6:30 the U.S.S. *Antares*—a repair ship towing a steel barge—was approaching the harbor entrance when she sighted a suspicious object, which looked like a midget submarine. The *Antares* immediately notified the *Ward*. At 6:33 a Navy patrol plane sighted the same object and dropped two smoke pots on the spot. The *Ward* hastened to the scene, spotting the sub—her superstructure just above the surface—at 6:40, and promptly opened fire. At the same time the patrol plane dropped bombs or depth charges. The submarine keeled over and began to sink, as the *Ward* dropped more depth charges. Shortly after 6:50 the destroyer sent a coded message that it had attacked a submarine in the defensive sea area.

At about 7:40 Admiral Kimmel received a telephone call from the staff duty officer, reporting the *Ward*-submarine incident. Kimmel replied, "I will be right down." Quickly he completed dressing and left for his headquarters.

Meanwhile, the Army's six mobile radar stations on Oahu had been on the alert since 4 A.M. in compliance

with General Short's Alert No. 1 instructions. At 7 A.M. five of these stations ceased operations, in accordance with these same instructions. At the remote Opana station at the northern tip of the island, Privates Joseph Lockard and George Elliott kept their set on while waiting for the truck which was to pick them up to take them to breakfast. Lockard, an experienced radar operator, planned to use this time to give Elliott a bit more instruction. At this moment an unusual formation appeared at the edge of the screen; Lockard checked the machine, found it operating properly, and at 7:02 A.M. concluded that a large number of aircraft, approximately 130 miles distant, was approaching Oahu from the north. For fifteen minutes Lockard and Elliott observed the approach of the formation, debating whether they should report it. Finally, at 7:20, Lockard called the radar information center. The switchboard operator informed him that the center had closed down twenty minutes before, that everyone had left except one Air Corps officer, First Lieutenant Kermet Tyler. Lockard reported the approaching flight to Tyler, who thought for a moment; the flight was undoubtedly either a naval patrol, a formation of Hickam Field bombers, or—most likely—a number of B-17's due from the mainland. "Forget it," he told Lockard.

Twenty minutes later—about 7:50—there was a bustle of activity on the decks of the ninety-four vessels of the Pacific Fleet in Pearl Harbor. It was almost time for morning colors on each vessel, and white-garbed sailors were briskly preparing for the daily flag-raising ceremony. Except for one destroyer, moving slowly toward the entrance, each ship was motionless at its moorings.

At 7:55 boatswains' whistles piped, and the preparatory signal for the colors ceremony was hoisted on each ship. At the same moment a low-flying plane, approaching over the hills to the northeast, swooped low over Ford Island, in the middle of the harbor. A bomb dropped on the seaplane ramp, close by the eight battleships moored next to the island. As the plane zoomed upward, displaying the red sun emblem of Japan, it was followed closely by others. By 9:45 some 260 Japanese planes had flashed that emblem over Oahu, and when the dreadful 110 minutes were over, 2,403 Americans—mostly sailors on the battleships—were dead or dying; 1,178 more had been wounded; the battle force of the Pacific Fleet had been destroyed, with four bat-

A West Point graduate and a combat veteran of the Burma campaign in World War II, Colonel Trevor N. Dupuy has devoted himself to writing on military subjects since his retirement from the Army in 1958.

tleships sunk or capsized and the remaining four damaged, while several smaller vessels were sunk or damaged severely. The Japanese lost twenty-nine planes, five midget submarines, and less than a hundred men.

One small further incident is pertinent to our assessment of United States leadership in high places just before Pearl Harbor.

The Nisei RCA messenger boy carrying General Marshall's message speedily found himself involved in trouble. Not until 11:45 could he thread his way through traffic jams, road blocks, and general confusion to reach the Fort Shafter signal office, which was itself swamped in traffic by this time.

Not until 2:58 P.M. Hawaiian time—9:58 that evening in bewildered Washington—was the message decoded and placed on Short's desk. He rushed a copy to Admiral Kimmel, who read it, remarked—perhaps unnecessarily—that it was not of the slightest interest any more, and dropped it into the wastebasket.

It had been a pretty long thirty minutes.

Who was responsible?

No disaster of the magnitude of Pearl Harbor could have occurred without the failure—somewhere and somehow—of leadership. A total of eight separate official investigations searched for scapegoats, and found them. The disaster remained a political football long after the last three of these investigations. And much confusion and argument still exist.

Yet through this welter of discord, some facts and conclusions stand out. Today, twenty years later, in another time of crisis, they hold important lessons.

It makes no difference, in assessing responsibility, that exceptional Japanese military skill, shrouded by deceit and assisted by almost incredible luck, accomplished its mission. Nor, indeed, does it matter that—as adjudicated in the always brilliant light of afterthought—Japan might well have inflicted defeat upon our Pacific Fleet and our Army forces in Hawaii regardless of how well alerted they may have been on December 7, 1941.

It makes no difference, so far as responsibility for the disaster itself was concerned, whether the war could have been prevented by wiser statesmanship or more astute diplomacy—though this would have required a wholehearted and unified national determination which did not exist in America in 1941 and the years before. It makes no difference that on December 7 the President and the Secretary of State—like the civilian Secretaries of War and Navy—had their eyes fixed on the Japanese threat in Southeast Asia. They had repeatedly warned the military men that war had probably become unavoidable.

What *does* matter is that the civilian statesmen—

however deft or clumsy, shrewd, or shortsighted—performed their difficult tasks of diplomacy and of administration confident that the military men would carry out their professional responsibilities by doing everything humanly possible to prepare for a war so clearly impending. They had every right to expect that—within the limits of scanty means available—the Armed Forces would be ready for any contingency.

The confidence and expectations of civilian leadership and of the nation were tragically dashed that Sunday morning twenty years ago.

Military failures were responsible for Pearl Harbor.

In Washington the most important of these were the following:

1. The War Department staff, over which General Marshall presided, was at the time a complicated but "one-man" shop, where delegation of responsibility was the exception rather than the rule. When Marshall was absent, the operational wheels tended to freeze. This situation was to some extent due to cumbersome organization, to some extent due to the personality of the Chief of Staff.

2. General Marshall, in a letter to General Short on February 7, 1941, stressed that "the risk of sabotage and the *risk involved in a surprise raid by air and submarine* [italics supplied] constitute the real perils of the [Hawaiian] situation." Yet, although definitely warning General Short on November 27 of the threat of war, and ordering him to report the measures he would take in response, Marshall did not check up on those measures; moreover, he was unaware that Short had done no more than to take routine precautions against sabotage. And General Gerow, heading the War Plans Division of General Marshall's General Staff—as he testified later in taking full responsibility for this slip—had not made any provision for following up operational orders. The net result was that both Marshall and Short remained the whole time in blissful ignorance of a vital misinterpretation of orders.

3. Marshall and Admiral Stark—and indeed all members of their staffs who knew the situation—permitted themselves to be hypnotized by the concrete evidence of the aggressive Japanese build-up in Southeast Asia which threatened our Philippines outpost. This theme, it will be remembered, ran as background to nearly all the warnings sent Hawaii. Thus succumbing to the illusory diagnosis of "enemy probable intentions," both top commanders ignored the danger implicit in our inability to locate at least four Japanese carriers.

4. Finally, on December 7, having indicated his full realization of the significance of the "one o'clock" intercept—that less than two hours now separated peace and war—and having decided not to use his "scrambler" telephone, Marshall failed to require surveillance and positive report on the delivery of his final warning.

These certainly were grave lapses in leadership. Yet in fairness, it should be noted that the consequences might not have been disastrous if all subordinate commanders had taken adequate security measures on the basis of the instructions, information, and warnings which they had received. To General Marshall's credit one must also chalk up his ability to profit by his mistakes. In less than three months after Pearl Harbor, he completely reorganized the War Department, decentralizing the mass of relatively minor administrative and executive matters that choked major strategical and tactical decisions. His newly created Operations Division of the General Staff—which he aptly termed his "command post"—ensured co-ordinated action and direction of Army activities in theaters of war all around the globe. On Oahu the situation was less ambiguous: military leadership at the top failed utterly.

Twenty years later, with war clouds again lowering over most of the world, the story of the Pearl Harbor disaster has more significance than mere passing memorials to the brave men who lost their lives that day. If the lessons are heeded, our surviving descendants may never again have to commemorate another "day of infamy."

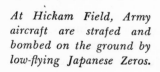

At Hickam Field, Army aircraft are strafed and bombed on the ground by low-flying Japanese Zeros.

"*Then and there the child Independence was born*"

CONTINUED FROM PAGE 39

ciliatory tone was the *quid pro quo* for his father's appointment is at best circumstantial, but informed people felt that the connection was obvious.

Otis pursued his irresolute, even self-contradictory course during the Stamp Act controversy. In his "Vindication of the British Colonies" he reversed his earlier position: Parliament *did* have the authority to impose taxes, he said, though he questioned whether the taxes imposed were fair. In two subsequent tracts he again shifted his ground. Arguing against the writs of assistance, he had decried laws enacted "by a foreign legislature, without our consent." Now he even accepted the theory of "virtual representation"—the fiction that the colonies were virtually represented in Parliament, in the sense that the interests of all Englishmen were theoretically represented by the whole body of Parliament—though propertyless subjects could not vote, though many Members represented "rotten boroughs," and though many English cities had no Member at all. "Representation," Otis conceded, "is now no longer a matter of right but of indulgence only." But in the second tract he swung completely around again, denied the right of taxation without representation, and demanded actual representation in Parliament.

Considering his erratic and equivocal wanderings, it is little wonder that when Otis ran again for the House he was attacked in a bit of doggerel appearing in the Boston *Evening Post* and attributed to a customs official not noted for his sobriety:

So Jemmy rail'd at upper folks *while Jemmy's Dad was out,*
But Jemmy's Dad has now a place, *so Jemmy's turn'd about. . . .*
And Jemmy is a silly dog, and Jemmy is a tool,
And Jemmy is a stupid cur, and Jemmy is a fool. . . .

The attack outraged the voters' sense of decency and "Jemmy" was elected to the House by a small majority. When he had thought himself ruined, Otis ruefully admitted, "the song of a drunkard saved me."

Sent as a Massachusetts delegate to the Stamp Act Congress in New York in 1765, Otis had the satisfaction of seeing his constitutional doctrine of no taxation without representation embodied in the Resolves adopted by that body. But the radical leaders refused to incorporate his demand for actual representation of the colonies in the House of Commons. Most of them were wary of a trap, for a grant of token representation to the colonies could not have checked the anticolonial course of the majority in Parliament.

Although far more moderate on the Stamp Act issue than either Patrick Henry or Daniel Dulany, Otis

plucked up his courage and under the pseudonym "John Hampden" published in the Boston press a sweeping denial of Parliament's right to tax the colonies. But by now his waverings had placed him under suspicion. Forced to defend himself at a Boston town meeting held in the spring of 1766, and to deny charges that his behavior was the result of "weak nerves" or "cowardice," he offered to meet George Grenville in single combat on the floor of Faneuil Hall to settle the whole issue. Again returned to the House with his popularity temporarily restored, Jemmy was humiliated when Governor Bernard vetoed his selection by his colleagues as Speaker as simply "impossible." Thenceforward for several years he collaborated with Sam Adams in directing the radical party in the House.

In February, 1768, Sam Adams drew up a circular letter denouncing Lord Townshend's external tax measures—import duties on such items as glass, lead, paper, and tea—enacted by Parliament. Lord Hillsborough, Secretary of State for the colonies, promptly denounced Adams' letter, ordered the Massachusetts legislature to rescind it, and instructed the colonial governors that the assemblies of other colonies be prevented, by dissolution if necessary, from endorsing it. Otis launched into an abusive two-hour tirade against Hillsborough, ridiculing king's ministers who, like Hillsborough, had been educated by travel on the European continent as "the very frippery and foppery of France, the mere outside of monkeys." Although he withheld criticism of George III, he delivered an encomium on Oliver Cromwell and defended the execution of Charles I. That same year, following the arrival in Boston of two regiments of redcoats, Otis wrote to an English correspondent:

You may ruin yourselves, but you cannot in the end ruin the colonies. Our fathers were a good people. We have been a free people, and if you will not let us remain so any longer, we shall be a great people, and the present measures can have no tendency but to hasten [with] great rapidity, events which every good and honest man would wish delayed for ages, if possible, prevented forever.

Unfortunately for his continued effectiveness as a political leader, no checkrein could be placed on Otis' abusive conduct toward others. "If Bedlamism is a talent, he has it in perfection," commented Tory Judge Peter Oliver, and even friendly critics agreed that Otis was unbalanced. The dispatch of troops to Boston heightened tempers. In 1769 Otis got into a coffeehouse brawl with John Robinson, a customs official. It is charitable to conclude that the caning he received accelerated his mental disintegration. In any event, two years later his family and friends requested he be examined by a sanity commission; as judge of probate, his old foe, Hutchinson, had the satisfaction of appointing its members, who found Otis to be a lunatic. Although he had intermittent lucid spells thereafter, he played no role at all during the Revolution. Instead, it was his brother Joseph who fought at Bunker Hill. James' death was appropriately dramatic. On May 23, 1783, he was standing in the doorway of a farmhouse in Andover when he was struck down by lightning. "He has been good as his word," commented Hutchinson. "Set the province in a flame and perished in the attempt."

A whole generation passed before John Adams, in a series of letters to the newspapers in 1818, established the legend of James Otis' heroic role. Even Virginians came to speak reverently of the "god-like Otis," and perhaps it is only fitting that he should be judged by his most brilliant and seminal achievement rather than by the sadder years when darkness fell upon him. It is only proper, too, that we recognize the writs of assistance case for what it was in fact—first of a series of crises which culminated at Lexington and Concord.

The attack against the writs, initiated by Otis, developed into a notable series of legal battles, fought not only in Massachusetts but throughout the colonies. Local justices of the peace in the Bay Colony refused in 1765 to grant them on the ground that they were repugnant to the common law. They continued to be issued by that province's Superior Court, but individuals sometimes managed to defy them: in 1766 a merchant named Daniel Malcolm, presumably on the advice if not at the instigation of Otis, refused to admit the customs officials into part of his cellar, even though they were armed with writs of assistance, and warned them that he would take legal action against them if they entered. The customs men backed down.

Meantime opposition to the writs was spreading to other colonies. In 1766 the customs collector of New London, Connecticut, sought legal advice as to his power of search and seizure, but the judges at New Haven felt that in the absence of a colonial statute they could make no determination. The collector referred the matter to the Commissioner of Customs in England, who in turn asked the advice of Attorney General William de Grey. His opinion came as a shock to the customs officials, for he found that the Courts of Exchequer in England "do not send their Processes into the Plantations, nor is there any Process in the plantations that corresponds with the description in the act of K[ing] W[illiam]."

Aware that the ground was now cut from under them, the Lords of Treasury saw to it that the Town-shend Acts passed in 1767 contained a clause specifically authorizing superior or supreme courts in the colonies to grant writs of assistance. Significantly, the American Board of Commissioners of Customs set up under the act sought between 1767 and 1773 to obtain writs in each of the thirteen colonies, but succeeded fully only in Massachusetts and New Hampshire. But as late as 1772 charges were made in Boston that "our houses and even our bed chambers are exposed to be ransacked, our boxes, chests, and trunks broke open, ravaged and plundered by wretches, whom no prudent man would venture to employ even as menial servants."

In other colonies the issue was stubbornly fought out in the courts. New York's Supreme Court granted the writs when the customs officers first applied for them in 1768, though not in the form the applications demanded; finally, the court flatly refused to issue the writs at all. In Pennsylvania the Tory Chief Justice, William Allen, refused also on the ground that it would be "of dangerous consequence and was not warranted by law." The writs were denied, too, in every southern colony save South Carolina, which finally capitulated and issued them in 1773. Significantly, the courts, though often manned by royal appointees, based their denials on the grounds advanced by Otis in the original Paxton case, going so far as to stigmatize the writs as unconstitutional.

What is important to remember throughout the controversy in which Otis played so large a part is that the colonists were seeking to define personal liberties—freedom of speech, the press, and religion—which even in England, right up to the eve of the American Revo-

Our Country, BY BENSON LOSSING

In February of 1761, just after his attack on the writs of assistance, the popular Otis was hailed by crowds in Boston.

lution, were not firmly enshrined in law. Indeed, the issues of whether a person could be arrested under a general warrant or committed to prison on any charge by a privy councillor were not settled until the 1760's. Then Lord Camden took a strong stand for freedom from police intrusion. Less dramatically perhaps than in the colonies, similar issues of civil liberties were being thrashed out in the mother country, but in the colonies this struggle laid the groundwork upon which the new Revolutionary states, and later the federal government, built their safeguards for civil liberties.

In Virginia, where the issue was contested most bitterly, writs of assistance were condemned in the Bill of Rights of June 12, 1776, as "grievous and oppressive." Condemnation was also reflected in the clauses in the Declaration of Independence denouncing the King because he had made judges dependent for their tenure and their salaries upon his will alone. Five other states soon followed Virginia in outlawing the writs. Of these, Massachusetts in her constitution of 1780 provided the most explicit safeguards. The relevant section of the state constitution, notable because it served as the basis for Madison's later incorporation of such a guarantee in the federal Bill of Rights, reads as follows:

XIV. Every subject has a right to be secure from all unreasonable searches and seizures of his person, his houses, his papers and all his possessions. All warrants, therefore, are contrary to this right, if the cause or foundation of them be not previously supported by oath or affirmation; and if the order in the warrant to a civil officer, to make search in suspected places, or to arrest one or more suspected persons, or to seize their property, be not accompanied with a special designation of the persons or objects of search, arrest, or seizure; and no warrant ought to be issued but in cases, and with the formalities prescribed by the laws.

John Adams, who wrote that constitution, had remembered his lessons very well indeed.

More succinctly than the guarantee in the Massachusetts constitution, the Fourth Amendment to the federal Constitution affirmed "the right of the people to be secure in their persons, houses, papers, and effects, against unreasonable searches and seizures," and declared that "no warrants shall issue, but upon probable cause, supported by oath or affirmation, and particularly describing the place to be searched, and the persons or things to be seized."

In our own day, several members of a Supreme Court heavily preoccupied with safeguarding personal liberty have conspicuously defended the guarantees in the Fourth Amendment. It was the late Justice Louis Brandeis who, in his dissenting opinion in a wiretapping decision of 1928 (*Olmstead v. U.S.*) opposing police intrusion without a search warrant, championed

"the right to be let alone—the most comprehensive of rights and the right most valued by civilized man. . . . To protect that right," he asserted, "every unjustifiable intrusion by the Government upon the privacy of the individual, whatever the means employed, must be deemed a violation of the Fourth Amendment."

More recently Justice Felix Frankfurter has opposed searches conducted as an incident to a warrant of arrest. In a notable dissent (*Harris v. U.S.*, 1946) he pointed out that the decision turned "on whether one gives the [Fourth] Amendment a place second to none in the Bill of Rights, or considers it on the whole a kind of nuisance, a serious impediment in the war against crime. . . . How can there be freedom of thought or freedom of speech or freedom of religion," he asked, "if the police can, without warrant, search your house and mine from garret to cellar merely because they are executing a warrant of arrest?" He went on to warn: "Yesterday the justifying document was an illicit ration book, tomorrow it may be some suspect piece of literature." Again, in a more recent case (*United States v. Rabinowitz*, 1950), Justice Frankfurter dissented from a decision authorizing federal officers to seize forged postage stamps without search warrant but as an incident to arrest. He said pointedly:

It makes all the difference in the world whether one recognizes the central fact about the Fourth Amendment, namely, that it was a safeguard against recurrence of abuses so deeply felt by the Colonies as to be one of the potent causes of the Revolution, or whether one thinks of it as merely a requirement for a piece of paper.*

Once it was a powerful monarch concerned about securing every shilling of customs revenue. Today it is a great republic legitimately concerned about the nation's security. Once it was the knock on the door. Today it is wire tapping or other electronic devices. The circumstances and techniques may differ. As the tragic James Otis would have realized, the issue remains the same.

Richard B. Morris is Gouverneur Morris professor of history at Columbia University, and editor of the John Jay Papers.

---

* In 1957 Mrs. Dollree Mapp of Cleveland, Ohio, was arrested for possessing obscene literature seized in her home by police, apparently without a warrant. Her subsequent conviction was upheld by two state appeal courts, but on June 19, 1961, the Supreme Court reversed the conviction, declaring that evidence obtained by search and seizure in violation of the Fourth Amendment is inadmissible in a state court, as it is in a Federal court. On the other hand, in the case of Burton N. Pugach of New York City, accused of conspiring to maim the girl who had rejected him, the Supreme Court on February 27, 1961, had upheld the right of state officials and state courts to use evidence obtained by wire tapping, a modern method of gathering evidence which many feel also violates a citizen's privacy. So the historic conflict between private right and the public good goes on.

Journey's End: 1865

CONTINUED FROM PAGE 35

Eight tall sergeants carried the coffin to the hearse, and the honor guard fell in behind. Drums throbbed and the procession moved through the bright May morning to the Statehouse. Ed Beall followed the casket in and took his position near its foot. He divided the crowd that came, sending them in two files, six abreast, past the dais where the coffin rested.

All that day and that night the lines moved through the Representative Hall. These were the folk from Lincoln's own country—from Petersburg, Jacksonville, Beardstown, Towanda, Metamora, Charleston; people who had known Lincoln the axeman, the boatman, the surveyor; people from the Eighth Circuit towns who had known Lincoln the lawyer, who had heard his drawling stories in the tavern and his arguments and summations in the courtrooms.

Among that endless line of mourners was lean, long-faced William H. Herndon. He had first seen Lincoln on a horseback trip along the Sangamon, when Lincoln was piloting the steamer *Talisman* over the ruined dam at New Salem. He had gone stump-speaking with him, had ridden with him on the circuit court, and had been his law partner for twenty-one years; their names were still together, "Lincoln & Herndon," on the office door now hung with crepe. During all that time they were "Billy" and "Mr. Lincoln," and now Bill Herndon stood with his own thoughts above the open coffin. "We who had known the illustrious dead in other days," he wrote, "and before the nation laid its claim upon him, moved sadly through and looked for the last time on the silent upturned face of our departed friend."

All night long the streets were thronged with people, as though no one could sink to rest, and church bells tolled hour after hour through the darkness. After a warm, windless night, the morning of May 4 brought a burning sunrise in a cloudless sky. It was the beginning of a blazing day—the hottest day ever known in Illinois, old residents said. By mid-morning hundreds were prostrated, and Mayor Dennis of Springfield had to be carried away from the crowded Statehouse square.

At noon a salute of twenty-one guns boomed through the hot, still air, and the final funeral procession formed. At the head were General Hooker and his staff; then Brigadier General Cook; Brigadier General Oakes; huge Justice Davis, whom Lincoln had appointed to the Supreme Court; Governor Yates of Illinois and his staff; the governors of other states; members of Congress; and a multitude of others. In the line was Old Tom, sweating under a caparison of black velvet, led by two perspiring grooms.

At Oak Ridge Bishop Matthew Simpson of the Methodist Church, a close friend of Lincoln's in Washington, gave a eulogy, and the massed choir sang in the blaze of sun. The coffins of Lincoln and his son Willie were placed in the hillside tomb. That small room was cool and dim, and it smelled of evergreens strewn on the stone floor.

Slowly the crowd dispersed. In the trance of heat Springfield grew quiet as the country town to which Lincoln had come nearly thirty years before. The congressmen went back to Washington. The governors returned to their capitals. By train, wagon, horseback, and on foot a multitude of people journeyed homeward. And from their assignment with history young Ed Beall went back to repairing boxcars and Bill Porter caught a freight on the Chicago and Alton run.

Professor Havighurst, of Miami University in Ohio, has written for this magazine on the Soo Canal and McGuffey's Readers. The article above will appear in his forthcoming book, The Heartland, *in Harper's Regions of America series.*

 *IF . . .*

An Enraged Actress.—Stanwix Hall, Albany, was the scene of what might have proved a tragedy a few days since. Miss Henrietta Irving—one of the Irving sisters—was the heroine of the affair. She entered the room of J. W. Booth, who was stopping at the Stanwix, and attacked him with a dirk, cutting his face badly. She did not, however, succeed in inflicting a mortal wound. Failing in this, she retired to her own room and stabbed herself. Again she failed in her destructive purpose. What promised to be a real tragedy in the outset was, after all, but a farce. The cause of this singular proceeding was attributed to jealousy or misunderstanding.

Richmond, Virginia, Daily Dispatch, *May 11, 1861*

full share of their votes, and together with the solid South and the "regular" Democrats of the North, this made an unbeatable combination.

The Bull Moosers were far from discouraged, however. Roosevelt ran a strong second, winning over 4,126,020 votes (to Wilson's 6,296,547) and carrying six states, including California, Michigan, and Pennsylvania. He overwhelmed Taft, despite all the President's advantages, so that the ample champion of the orthodoxy won only 3,486,720, or eight electoral votes.* The future looked bright. "Progressive seed has been sewn on such a large area of soil that a pretty fair crop is bound to be the result ere long," Perkins announced after the election.

But there was much to learn about politics, Perkins had discovered. Selling a candidate was not like hawking insurance. Some of the personal qualities that had made him a brilliant businessman proved only weaknesses when applied to politics. He found it impossible to subordinate himself to a team effort. The *Bulletin* had been his idea, and a good one, but he had made it far too much a vehicle for *his* views rather than for general Progressive policies and opinions. The first issue contained a full-page reprint of an editorial in the New York *Journal* praising his organizing ability. Two weeks later there was a long account of a petty argument between Perkins and Woodrow Wilson over the difference between Tammany Society and Tammany Hall. Two issues later came a lead article by Perkins on Wilson and the trust question.

It was natural enough for the *Bulletin* to stress the trust issue; it was central to Perkins' beliefs, and by 1912 Roosevelt was substantially in accord with Perkins' idea that government regulation was the proper way to deal with giant corporations. But Perkins erred deeply when he allowed the *Bulletin* to devote such a disproportionate amount of space to the question and to print his name as often as it did. His aggressiveness irritated many loyal Progressives. The conservation expert Gifford Pinchot, for example, dubbed him "Gabby George," and another supporter of T.R. claimed that the entire New York organization of the party "consisted of George W. Perkins and a push button." Such criticism came as a profound shock to the political neophyte.

Another lesson that Perkins had to learn during the campaign was that the rough and tumble of politics is not for the tender-skinned. He had given up all his

profitable business connections—his partnership in the Morgan firm alone was probably worth a million dollars a year—in order to work for public betterment. He believed utterly in the soundness of his crusade against the Sherman Antitrust Act; certainly no one should question his motives, he thought. He had remained active in U.S. Steel and in International Harvester not to make money, for he drew no salary from either company, but because he felt that "these organizations are right from the viewpoint of modern ethics, just as I am sure they are necessary from the viewpoint of modern economics." Yet now he found himself assailed as an unscrupulous and selfish capitalist seeking to use the government to benefit his pet monopolies.

Scarcely had Roosevelt been nominated by the Progressives when a Democratic congressman began to call Perkins "the chief intermediary" between big business and the Justice Department, the "minister plenipotentiary and envoy extraordinary" of the Morgan interests. Even Woodrow Wilson, who did not stoop to mudslinging, was unusually forthright in attacking Perkins and his views. "These gentlemen say that these big combinations are necessary for economy and efficiency," Wilson said in one speech. "The only answer I can think of that meets the suggestion is: Rats! Go tell all that to the Marines."

Perkins was naturally angered by these criticisms, most of which questioned not only his beliefs but also his motives. It was particularly exasperating to be called a tool of the House of Morgan when in fact J. P. Morgan, Jr., was trying to force him off the Board of Directors of U.S. Steel! Morgan thought Perkins' political activities "controversial" and likely to injure the corporation. Many other business leaders, of course, were horrified by Perkins' views on government regulation of business, which they considered socialistic.

Perkins did not resign from U.S. Steel, then or later, nor did he alter his basic beliefs. Nevertheless, when the campaign was over he changed his political techniques considerably in the light of his 1912 experiences. He made an effort to conciliate Progressives, like Gifford and Amos Pinchot, who had criticized his leadership. In part the objections of these men had been ideological, for they were ardent advocates of trust busting. (Amos Pinchot once tried to write a book exposing the sins of U.S. Steel.) The party structure was revamped and critics of Perkins given important places in it. The *Bulletin* was transferred to other hands, both the trust question and Perkins' name disappearing from its pages. A Progressive Service, to pro-

* In this election, the Socialist Eugene V. Debs received about 900,000 votes, the highest percentage of the total vote that party ever won.

vide economic and sociological information useful in drafting legislation, was established.

Nevertheless, even his co-workers found it hard to accept Perkins' leadership. Prejudices rising from his former business connections would not die down. "Perkins stands for nothing but rights of property," a disgruntled Progressive from South Dakota complained. Nor could Perkins completely suppress what William Allen White called his "seven-devil lust to grab the drum and get up around to the head of the procession." The business world had taught him to act decisively, but not how to give others a sense of participation.

It is extremely significant that, in Perkins, leadership looked more and more like dictatorship. Roosevelt started a third party because he felt that a small clique of professionals had stolen control of the G.O.P. Yet from start to finish, the Progressive organization itself was managed by a tiny inner circle. In the summer of 1912, delegates to the first Progressive convention were hand-picked by local caucuses in the traditional smoke-filled rooms; at the climactic 1916 convention, Perkins and a few other leaders intrigued for days to prevent the delegates from nominating Roosevelt before the Republican convention had committed itself, although nearly every soul among them desired to do so at once. It was the methods, not the program, that soured the rank and file.

Of course there were other reasons why Roosevelt's Bull Moose organization did not fulfill the high hopes of 1912 in succeeding years. Wilson's New Freedom undermined the Progressive appeal by putting many of its proposals into effect. And the party lacked the patronage, prestige, and organization at the grass roots to sustain itself while out of power. Its one matchless asset was Roosevelt, yet after the outbreak of the European war the old Rough Rider rapidly lost interest in domestic affairs. First enthusiasm faded, then hope. By 1916 many Progressives were ready to go back to the Republicans on almost any terms. One of Perkins' strengths was his continuing willingness to contribute time and money to the cause when others drifted away.

The story of the efforts of Progressive and Republican leaders to agree upon a common candidate in 1916 has already been told in these pages (see "T.R. on the Telephone," AMERICAN HERITAGE, December, 1957). Perkins arranged for the then-novel private telephone that connected the politicians in Chicago with Roosevelt in Oyster Bay, and paid the bill. But his main role was to keep the Progressives quiet until the Republicans could be persuaded to accept the apostate Roosevelt as their candidate. When compromise efforts failed, and when Roosevelt decided to support the Republican nominee, Charles Evans Hughes, Perkins

NEW YORK *Telegram*, AUGUST 5, 1912

Newspapers lampooned Perkins and publisher Frank Munsey for their support of T. R.'s Bull Moose revolt.

went along with him reluctantly; personally he had little use for Hughes.

The Progressives now disappeared as a party, and Roosevelt, the leader, devoted himself chiefly to assailing Wilson's foreign policy. Perkins, on the other hand, was determined to keep fighting for the Progressive program within the Republican ranks. He persuaded Hughes to include six former Progressives—including himself—on the Republican campaign committee. Later, after Hughes' narrow defeat of 1916, when the Old Guard seized control of the Republican Executive Committee, Perkins tried to organize a liberal revolt, an effort cut short by U.S. entry into the European war. The following year Perkins led the battle that resulted in the election of Will Hays, who was friendly to the former Progressives, as Republican National Chairman. It was in no small part because of Perkins that the Old Guard faction was held in check until the 1920 election. By that time Perkins was no longer alive to fight.

Unlike so many amateur politicians, Perkins was willing to work as hard on local and state questions as on "important" national problems. The 1915 revision of the New York State constitution (which he opposed) and the wartime New York City Food Committee (which he managed) are examples of his activities on these levels. In 1914 he traveled all the way to the Panama Canal Zone simply to try to persuade Colonel George W. Goethals, the engineer in charge of constructing the canal, to accept appointment as New

York City Police Commissioner. Goethals did not come.

Perkins' governing principle, in local and national politics and in business too, was that the people, if given a chance to understand fully, would always do whatever was right. This faith in democracy was typically "Progressive"—Bryan, it will be recalled, possessed it so utterly that he assumed automatically that the truth could be determined by counting noses. What distinguished Perkins' faith in the people was his willingness to invest vast amounts of his own money in seeing that the public was fully informed. When he was battling for stricter food and price controls during the war, he spent thousands spreading his views.

His dedication to Jefferson's great principle that the truth, if left to itself, would always prevail, was proved conclusively by an incident that occurred during the fight. He was challenged by Samuel Fraser of the New York Federation of Farm Bureaus. Perkins, Fraser said, was making unfair use of his wealth by flooding the state with huge advertisements which his opponent could not afford to match. Without a moment's hesitation, Perkins offered to buy space in every paper in the state so that Fraser could present his arguments to the people. On September 27, 1917, Fraser's indictment of Perkins was spread across the pages of 141 New York newspapers, at a cost to Perkins of $25,000.

This use of widespread advertising for political purposes was a new thing. Perkins, the trade paper *Editor and Publisher* commented in 1915, had "uncovered the 42-centimeter gun that from now on must be considered the master of the situation when it comes to carrying the redoubts of public opinion." In all his political activities, as earlier in business, he was noted for boldness, imagination, and a willingness to use new and unconventional methods. When battling to keep down New York food prices in 1917, he discovered that there was a great run of smelts on the Pacific coast and bought over 100,000 pounds at four cents a pound. These he shipped to New York and sold to retailers at four and a half cents, on condition that they sell them to the public for not more than six. At that moment, Atlantic coast smelts were selling at about eighteen cents a pound.

The Great War affected Perkins profoundly, although not really until it was all over. Like any public-spirited citizen he worked hard during the conflict—at his Food Committee job and in raising money for the Y.M.C.A. But two events in late 1918 hit him with staggering force. One was the death of his son's young wife in the flu epidemic. The other was an investigation he made of Y.M.C.A. activities overseas right after the Armistice. His experiences in France and Germany broadened and tempered his Progressiv-

ism. When first he saw the devastated areas of France he had seethed with rage against the Germans. But anger and revenge were futile in the face of so much misery and destruction.

When he stepped off the boat on his return to America, he told reporters that economic reconstruction seemed far more urgent than political. They asked him about the menace of Russian communism, and he said: "I don't know what to say about Bolshevism in Europe. There are deep-seated troubles there. In Paris . . . people are paying $1 apiece for apples, and $3 a pound for butter." When asked if, by feeding Russians and Germans, the Allies were not "nursing a viper in the breast," he replied: "How are we going to cut out any one group of people?"

Realizing that the world was at a great turning point, Perkins searched hard for the path that "the man of the future" should take through the morass of postwar readjustment. There was much labor unrest; a bitter strike was convulsing the steel industry; and angry radicals were talking of sweeping changes in the order of things. "The questions that took me out of the banking business," Perkins wrote his old friend Albert J. Beveridge, "are now coming to a head." In December, 1919, in a lecture at Columbia University, he argued that the politicians of the future must "so frame our laws as to permit co-operative effort . . . conducted under proper regulation and control."

Where national politics was concerned, Perkins was moved by the same vague and somewhat authoritarian desire to get at fundamentals and by a conviction that intense partisanship was out of place in modern society. When one politician suggested to him that the trend was running so strongly toward the Republicans that they could elect a "yellow dog" President in 1920, he replied by asking him icily "what use . . . a yellow dog would be to our country and the world at large in the handling of the momentous questions presenting themselves at this time." And he lectured Senator Reed Smoot of Utah about the importance of "constructive thought" and the futility of "hot-air speeches."

Such words had little effect on Smoot and the other leaders of the Republican party, who were then not at all interested in Perkins' ideas about "proper regulation and control" of the economy. They gave the country Warren G. Harding and "normalcy." But Perkins did not live to see what followed, for his health failed rapidly in the spring of 1920, and in June he died, victim of acute encephalitis complicated by a heart condition.

George Perkins had brains, money, enthusiasm, self-confidence, and faith in the cause of reform. Even his enemies acknowledged his winning nature, his sincerity, his vivacity. "Anyone who knows him cannot help liking him," his relentless foe Amos Pinchot confessed. Why then did he fail at reform? In part, the prejudices of lesser men undid him: they called him a tool of the "interests." "If I had built a hospital . . . or endowed a library with the money I spent," he told one critic toward the end of his career, "many people would have risen up and called me blessed . . . I prefer to spend what money I am able in advancing measures that I believe are thoroughly in the public interest, and I intend to pursue this course."

But Perkins was also partially responsible for his own failure. He was too headstrong to be successful in politics. His decisiveness and his dedication often led him to ignore others. When called to account, he liked to reply that every business must have a single head, and he could cite examples from his experience in industry to prove his point. The real nature of political democracy still escaped him: this was the paradox of Perkins' life. He believed that progress depended upon men learning to work together, but he could not work in harness with others at the task of making a better world.

The Legend Maker CONTINUED FROM PAGE 59

will sell like flax seed at a quarter of a dollar. I cou'd make you a world of pence and popularity by it."

Neither Carey with hardheaded business calculation nor the irrepressible Parson in his most flamboyant dream could have foreseen the success and impact on the American people that Weems' *The Life and Memorable Actions of George Washington* would achieve. In scarcely more than a century and a half it has gone through eighty-two known editions, including translations into French and German. The last edition appeared in 1927. During the author's lifetime, eighteen editions were exhausted, six of which disappeared "like flax seed" in the first five years. It was in the fifth edition that Weems added the cherry tree story. In 1806, inspired by the rapid sale of four editions, he revised and enriched his little volume with many "new and valuable anecdotes," and jacked the price from twenty-five cents to half a dollar a copy. Most of the more famous stories of Washington's youth first appeared in this edition.

Parson Weems himself is something of a legend, for there are few authentic facts about his early life, and many stories. He was born October 11, 1759, the nineteenth child of David Weems, who lived on his farm, Marshes Seat, near Herring Bay in Anne Arundel County, Maryland. He was not long to suffer the chores of farm life, because before he reached his teens his father sent him away to school. The young student was diligent in his courses and early showed a zest for sharing his knowledge. For hours during the week young Weems disappeared from school, and no one knew where he went until he was discovered, not playing hookey, but teaching the poor. He was a born preacher but seems to have tried other professions before he found his vocation. He took several trips on his two older brothers' trading vessels, but the life of a sailor did not appeal to him. When the Revolution broke out, young Weems was in Edinburgh, Scotland, apparently (for there is no record) studying medicine and surgery. In 1779 his father died, leaving him a part of the estate and some slaves. The story goes that the young student returned to his embattled country long enough to secure his inheritance, free his slaves, and receive a call to the ministry in the Anglican Church.

About 1780 (the date is uncertain) Weems sailed back to England for seminary training, but when he was ready for ordination he ran into difficulty. As a good American he refused to acknowledge the supremacy of King George III, and the English bishops refused to ordain him. With England's recognition of American independence, however, the Church relented, and the Archbishop of Canterbury ordained Weems without the distasteful oath of supremacy.

As a preacher Weems was highly successful with the people and continually in hot water with disapproving Episcopal clergymen. His methods were unorthodox and his ideas disturbingly liberal. In 1784 he took an appointment as rector of All Hallows Church near his home on Herring Creek. The parish covered a large rural area, and one of Weems' duties was to minister to the needs of outlying villages. He worked hard, preaching wherever he could gather a crowd, in a field or in a ballroom—"like a Methodist," some of his colleagues grumbled. He actively opposed slavery, a position not pleasing to some of the wealthy slave-holding vestrymen. His bubbling humor crept into his sermons, which some thought lacked dignity and smacked of sin. He also loved to play the fiddle. In 1789, perhaps for some or all of these reasons, he was relieved of his parish. While he served two others in 1791 and 1792, he now began to reprint and sell volumes of sermons for extra income, and by 1794 had left the ministry as a profession forever—but not before scandalizing a clerical convention by reprinting and selling there a medical pamphlet on abnormal sex habits.

Although Weems could never stop preaching, his primary occupation from 1794 until his death in 1825 was that of bookseller and author. Loaded with books, he rode in his Jersey wagon over the highways and byways of the upper South, undaunted by "roads horrid and suns torrid," or by the seasons of mud, dust, and snow. He became a familiar figure at village fairs, and welcome company at lonely farms as well as at big plantations. He pictured himself to Mathew Carey, who supplied him with books, as a penniless vagabond but tireless worker, referring to himself as "ragged Mother Carey's chicken." Certainly he gave the appearance of a rootless itinerant peddler as he rattled along the rutted roads, a quill pen stuck in his hat, a little inkhorn dangling from the large lapel of his clerical coat, his hair flowing down to his shoulders, and a bookcase sticking up in the wagon behind him. But he was far from the ordinary peddler; as a good southerner, he claimed noble English blood, married Frances Ewell, a well-bred Virginia girl, and settled in a substantial house called Bel Air in Dumfries, Virginia. He traveled much, selling a large share of his cultural merchandise himself, but he also had agents in Maryland, Virginia, the Carolinas, and Georgia hawking his wares for him.

As a salesman Weems pioneered in the techniques later so successfully developed by the Fuller Brush Company and the denizens of Madison Avenue. He knew his market well—the rural South—and he knew its people and their psychology. "There is a time," he once advised Carey, "to catch popular feelings as well as young Rabbits & a cold cloudy day is not that time—a warm bright day is the thing." The southerners Weems knew were, for the most part, barely literate back-country farmers, some of whom had carved their land out of the wilderness. They wrestled no holds barred, ran foot races, drank prodigious quantities of raw whiskey, and hunted possum. They took pride in their independence, bowing to no man. They were not virtuous but had a fixed idea of virtue, and, since most of them knew that they fell far short of the mark, they sought to save their souls at those emotional orgies, the revivalist camp meetings. They were loyal to their families, patriotic about their states, and fiercely proud of their new country.

Like modern brand-name companies, Weems sold himself first and then his products. Often he was invited to preach in the village church; the denomination never mattered, for the dauntless Parson now preached a universal morality, and even, said some of his clerical critics, used the pulpit to hawk his wares. Whether this be calumny or truth, the fact is that he often served as a guest preacher before vending his wares. The testimonial, too, was a tool in the Parson's

sales kit. On two occasions, for instance, he got Washington himself to endorse reprinted moral tracts.

No amount of prestige and good public relations, however, would induce people to buy something that they did not need or desire. Weems knew the tastes of his people. His letters to Mathew Carey are filled with urgent requests for popular volumes, such as William Guthrie's *A New System of Modern Geography* or Oliver Goldsmith's *An History of the Earth and Animated Nature*. He begged for speedy delivery of one hundred copies of Guthrie

e'er the Infant Boreas has had time to muster his tremendous forces and let me entreat thee, my dear Fellow Democrat, by our mutual friendships and our mutual interests to lend the *swiftest wings* to those Goldsmiths. . . . And the sooner thou sendest them the better, for how canst thou send them in the Winter when every wind is a storm and every wave running mountain high threatens destruction to the laboring barque?

The Bible, however, was his staple, and he was constantly urging Carey to publish a large, handsomely bound edition which he promised would quickly find a prominent place in every farmhouse in the South. Moral tracts he sold by the thousands. These were cheap little pamphlets that illustrated the rewards of virtue and the penalties of vice, with far more elaborate descriptions of vice than of virtue. Many of these tracts were the products of Weems' own pen (*see page 93*).

The jolly book-peddler tried not to miss a court day, when the dusty country roads were jammed with farm wagons headed for the village, bustling with activity as the judge, lawyers, and clerks moved into the local courthouse. Farmers and their families broke rural routine, flocking to town to join the festivities, to settle legal matters, to watch the trials, to buy and to sell, to exchange gossip with friends, and to have a good time. On those days, "when the spirits of the People shall be getting gay and bold," Parson Weems was at his best. He would rise with the sun, bathe (an eccentricity in that day of no hot and cold running water) in a cool stream outside the village, then dress and drive his book-laden wagon to town. On such occasions he often sold a thousand or more books and pamphlets; that is, if Carey sent a sufficient number of the right titles—the ones Weems demanded, not the ones the publisher wished sold.

Mathew Carey and his impish bookseller rarely agreed on anything, and theirs was a tempestuous relationship. Carey was a hot-tempered Irish Catholic. Born in Dublin in 1760, he agitated against British rule of Ireland, whereupon a price was put upon his head. He escaped to France, where Benjamin Franklin gave him a job in a printing plant he had set up at Passy. But shortly Carey was back in Dublin again, editing an anti-British journal. He served a brief term in jail and then, again threatened with imprisonment, disguised himself as a woman and boarded a ship for America. In Philadelphia, the young fugitive founded in 1785 the firm of Carey and Lea, now the oldest publishing house in North America, although altered to Lea and Febiger. Carey very quickly made his the leading concern in the country, although, as Weems often reminded him, he owed a part of this success to the salesmanship and literary talent of his southern agent. Carey, however, would never admit this to Weems, whom he considered unbusinesslike, if not unreliable. He was constantly after Weems to write to him more often, to let him know where he was and what he was doing. The Parson, on his side, upbraided Carey for sending him unsalable volumes— Goethe, for example—when he had asked for elegantly bound books of travel for the libraries of the Virginians, light reading for the Georgians and the Carolinians, and more Bibles, moral tracts, and textbooks.

They could be breezy with one another as well. Thus Weems to Carey: "How long, thou eldest born of confusion, how long wilt thou continue to send the books to South James River, and the *invoice* to the headwaters of the Patomak? Would God thou woudst always suffer the invoice to sleep in peace in the same trunk that contains the books!" Carey, replying, complained: "My Friend and fellow citizen, your *volume* bearing the date of the twelfth instant and covering a note for 100 dollars (I expected three) I received an hour ago. I am surprised you stayed so short a time and did so little at Fredericksburg."

During the course of their association Weems quit several times in disgust, whereupon Carey would fire him in a rage, as in October, 1796, when Carey roasted Weems again for not writing.

You are not the first person I have met with, forward to throw the blame of his own misconduct on Guiltless Shoulders. Whatever disappointments you have met with in the requisite supplies, you may charge to a pretty large A/C [account], viz, that of your neglect of writing & informing me of your route. Had you done on the subject as I so often importuned you to do, you would have ample provision everywhere before you. . . .

The following spring, Carey was fed up and terminated the relationship. "I wish to prevent your journey to Richmond, and any other journey for me as long as you live. I wish no further dealings with a man, who while he can cant for hours about morals and religion is as insatiable and griping as the harpy Shylock. . . ." The summer, however, found Carey visiting Weems at Dumfries, and the reunion was so pleasant that Weems

forgot to discuss some business details, for, he said later, "being in company with Mathew Carey, Esq. I had no faculty but for chat and laughter." But in January of 1810 they were hard at it again. A speculative venture failed, and Carey blamed Weems. Weems replied:

Now in God Almighty's name! what ground had I from all this to infer that you were going to borrow 20 thousand dollars from the bank. . . . Yes sir, for a long time you have done nothing but *slander* and *trouble* me who can now with honest joy defy you in the presence of God to say when did I ever rob you of one penny, or when did I ever hold back one penny of what belonged to you. You are constantly telling me what great wealth I might have made in your employ, but what would be all the wealth in this world made in the service of an unreasonable and inhuman taskmaster who makes no allowances for delays . . .

Yet, by the end of the month, Weems was admonishing Carey,

this is no time to write intemperate letters. And you ought, and I doubt not, will one day blush for what you have written. You see that notwithstanding your indecent reflections on my "*honor*," I am constantly sending you monies, and I may add *large* monies, which it is remembered that I have a *very limited variety indeed* of your books and of these many not very salable . . .

And so it went on to a new rupture. But always they renewed their relationship as if nothing had happened.

In this anguished manner Weems made his living, but it was as the author of historical biography that he won immortality. Historians and critics have either turned aside the Parson's work as unimportant, or have damned it as unreliable, and thus his role in American letters and mythology is little understood. What Weems did was to make national symbols of his subjects, legendary giants of republican virtue and bravery for a hero-starved people, heroes of recent history for a people cut off by their own volition from their heroes of legend.

Heroes represent the ideals of a people—what should be, not what is or was. In 1800 the United States was still a very young nation with as yet only one great national event, the Revolution, an experience shared by the whole country. The republic possessed but few of the symbols that serve to evoke patriotism; it had a flag but no anthem; a Fourth of July, but no other national holiday; no national monuments, no shrines. There were no precedents to follow, no examples that seemed to apply. Americans had to create their own heroes, and for this task Weems was eminently well fitted.

Without a hint of a change of pace, Weems could write a moral tirade or a biography. Very often he seemed to alternate between the two, but upon close examination it becomes almost absurdly obvious that this is not the case—all of Weems' works are the same! They are dressed differently and the words are not the same, but under the surface they are all alike in one important respect: they are all moral tracts. And this is precisely what the Parson intended them to be, for he was a bookseller and a minister, not a historian or even a biographer. His purpose was to make money from his work and to furnish his readers with strong arguments and examples for following the paths of virtue and shunning the lures of vice. He was not interested in teaching readers history or in probing the real motivations of the great. He used the lives of famous men, of Washington, Francis Marion, Franklin, and Penn, simply for illustration. By Weems' simple formula—later adapted by William H. McGuffey in his *Readers* and Horatio Alger in his rags-to-riches stories—men are successful, in any field of endeavor, only in proportion to the amount of virtue that they display in their everyday living.

Weems picked Benjamin Franklin early as one of his heroes, "the great economist of America" and symbol of monetary success. In 1797 he published a book of selections from *Poor Richard's Almanac* called *The Immortal Mentor; or Man's Unerring Guide to a Healthy, Wealthy, and Happy Life,* but it wasn't until 1815 that he published his biography of Franklin. The biography is not very good, not even up to Weems' standard. Perhaps the worldly side of Franklin was too much even for the Parson.

The Life of William Penn, too, was a later production, in 1822. The clerical biographer portrayed the adventurous Quaker as a pudgy, pious, and benevolent burgher who refuses King Charles II's offer of soldiers on an expedition to the New World. He displays a stubborn faith that the Indians share the "moral sense" bestowed on all men by the grace of God. Weems records this interesting exchange between Charles II and William Penn when Charles objects, "I fear, friend William, that that grace has never appeared to the Indians of North America."

"Why not to them as well as to all others!"

"If it had appeared to them, they would hardly have treated my subjects so barbarously as they have done."

"That's no proof to the contrary, friend Charles. Thy subjects were the aggressors." [Penn then describes the Indians as the kindest creatures in the world and explains that he intends to buy their lands, not to seize them.]

[The King, surprised, says,] "Buy their lands of them! why, man, you have already bought them of me."

"Yes, I know I have; and at a dear rate too: but I did it only to get thy *good will,* not that I thought thou hadst any *right* to their lands."

"Zounds, man! no right to their lands!"

"No, friend Charles, no right at all. What right hast thou to their lands?"

"Why, the right of discovery. . . ."

"The right of *discovery!*" replied William Penn, half smiling, "a strange kind of right indeed! Now suppose, friend Charles, some canoe loads of these Indians, crossing the sea, and *discovering* thy island of Great Britain, were to claim it as their own, and set it up for sale over thy head, what wouldst thou think of it?"

"Why—why—why," replied Charles, blushing, "I must confess I should think it a piece of great impudence in them."

"Well, then, how canst thou, a CHRISTIAN, and a CHRISTIAN PRINCE too, do that which thou so utterly condemnest in these people whom thou callest SAVAGES?"

The king was "rather too much staggered to make a reply." Weems quickly points the moral and hopes "that the AMERICAN YOUTH will take notice how very small indeed, a wicked king appears when placed by the side of an honest man."

Next in merit and popularity to Weems' *Life of Washington* is his *Life of General Francis Marion,* which was actually ghostwritten by Weems. One of Marion's companions-in-arms, General Peter Horry, had intended to write a biography, but was unable to put it together and gave Weems the material. Later Weems was forced to acknowledge his authorship when the outraged Horry repudiated the published work as a "military romance." Weems pictured Marion as the courageous, dashingly romantic "Swamp Fox" whose republican virtues enabled him to outwit Britain's finest generals. The book is as much a tale of the adventures of Marion's men as of the wily Swamp Fox himself, filled with stories of their feats—tales which have become a part of our Revolutionary tradition (*see* "The Elusive Swamp Fox," AMERICAN HERITAGE, April, 1958).

Colorful as the adventures of Marion were, the book never rivaled *The Life of Washington* in quality or popularity. George Washington as a moral example served Weems' purposes best. Here was a Virginia aristocrat who had married wealth, increased it through land speculation, won the war, and become first President. Was this not an example seemingly impossible of emulation by the common youth, who could scarcely hope "to be called to direct the storm of war, or to ravish the ears of deeply listening Senates?" But the Parson assured his young audience that it was not these public acts nor the advantages of wealth that made Washington great. No, it was private virtues that exalted him to be *"Columbia's first and greatest son."* And therefore, concluded Weems, "every youth may become a Washington . . ."

DRUNKARDS BEWARE!

THE
DRUNKARD'S LOOKING GLASS,

REFLECTING A FAITHFUL

LIKENESS OF THE DRUNKARD,

IN

SUNDRY VERY INTERESTING ATTITUDES,

WITH

*Lively Representations of the many strange Capers which he cuts at
different Stages of his Disease;*

AS FIRST,

WHEN HE HAS ONLY "A DROP IN HIS EYE;"

SECOND,

WHEN HE IS "HALF SHAVED;"

THIRD,

WHEN HE IS GETTING "A LITTLE ON THE STAGGERS OR SO;"

AND FOURTH AND FIFTH, AND SO ON,

TILL HE IS "QUITE CAPSIZED;"

OR

"SNUG UNDER THE TABLE WITH THE DOGS,'

AND *CAN*

"STICK TO THE FLOOR WITHOUT HOLDING ON."

BY M. L. WEEMS,
Author of the Life of Washington, &c.

SIXTH EDITION, GREATLY IMPROVED

PRINTED FOR THE AUTHOR.
1818.
(Price Twenty-five Cents)

GOD'S REVENGE

AGAINST

ADULTERY,

AWFULLY EXEMPLIFIED IN THE FOLLOWING CASES

OF

AMERICAN CRIM. CON.

I. THE ACCOMPLISHED DR. THEODORE WILSON, (DELAWARE,) WHO FOR SEDUCING
MRS. NANCY WILEY, HAD HIS BRAINS BLOWN OUT
BY HER HUSBAND.

II. THE ELEGANT JAMES O'NEALE, ESQ. (NORTH CAROLINA,) WHO FOR SEDUCING
THE BEAUTIFUL MISS MATILDA L'ESTRANGE, WAS KILLED
BY HER BROTHER.

BY MASON L. WEEMS,
AUTHOR OF THE LIFE OF WASHINGTON.

THIRD EDITION

PHILADELPHIA

PRINTED FOR THE AUTHOR—PRICE 25 CENTS.

1818.

GRIGG & CO. PRINTERS.

THE PIOUS PAMPHLETS
OF PARSON WEEMS

*The star book salesman peddled his own tracts. One
case history in "The Drunkard's Looking Glass" told how
tipsy young Dred Drake (above, left) met a bloody end.
The hapless adulterer at right below is Theodore Wilson, shown getting his just deserts from an irate husband.*

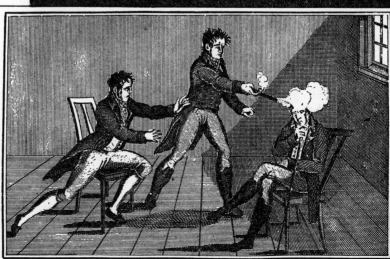

There! G__d d__n you take that!

Weems' object was hardly absolute truth. In January, 1800, the puckish Parson wrote Carey, "I've something to whisper in your lug. Washington, you know is gone! Millions are gaping to read something about him. I am very nearly prim^d and cock^d for 'em." He then outlined his biography of Washington and told Carey that "I . . . show that his unparalleled rise & elevation were owing to his Great Virtues. 1 His Veneration for the Deity or Religious Principles. 2 His Patriotism. 3 His Magnanimity. 4 His Industry. 5 His Temperance & Sobriety. 6 His Justice &c. &c. Thus I hold up his great Virtues . . . to the imitation of Our Youth. All this I have lin^d and enliven^d with Anecdotes apropos interesting and entertaining."

Under Weems' moralistic pen the boy became an impossible prig, the general an incarnation of the war god, and President Washington an American Solomon. As a lad, according to his biographer, Washington not only did not lie, but he also abhorred fighting and would not tolerate it among his schoolmates. "If he could not disarm their savage passions by his arguments, he would instantly go to the master, and inform him of their barbarous intentions." As a general, too, Washington was absolutely unmatched. Finally, as President, according to his enthusiastic biographer, Washington with wisdom and justice exalted "his country from the brink of infamy and ruin to the highest ground of prosperity and honour, both at home and abroad. . . ."

Later, as the Parson's little biography reached a popularity far beyond his fondest dreams, he began to realize what he had created. In 1809 Weems wrote President Jefferson that he had not set Washington up "as a Common Hero for military ambition . . . to idolize and imitate—nor an Aristocrat, . . . to mislead and enslave, but a pure Republican whom all our youth should know that they may imitate his virtues and thereby immortalize 'the last Republic now on earth'. . . ." Weems was not alone in raising Washington to the position of a demigod in the public mind. Gilbert Stuart's stiff, pale portrait has become the official likeness, and Jared Sparks, who edited the first edition of Washington's letters, changed pungent phrases and tough language to the stilted style befitting the man in Stuart's portrait and the image of Weems' virtuous hero.

The ruddy portraits of the Peales may be substituted for Stuart's work on official seals and stamps, and Washington's own language has been restored in subsequent editions of his letters, but as long as Washington's birthday is celebrated, Weems' anecdotes will be retold. The little Parson who set out to make some money and strike a blow for morality married Washington forever to that hatchet and that cherry tree, and he created an image of our first national hero that has become a permanent part of America's heritage.

David D. Van Tassel is associate professor of American Intellectual History at the University of Texas and the author of Recording America's Past: An Interpretation of the Development of Historical Studies in America, 1607–1884, *published by the University of Chicago Press in 1960.*

For further reading: Parson Weems of the Cherry Tree, *by Harold Kellock (Century, 1928);* Parson Weems, *by Lawrence C. Wroth (Baltimore, 1911); and* Three Discourses, *by Mason L. Weems, Emily E. F. Skeel, Ed. (Random House, 1927).*

How We Got Guantanamo CONTINUED FROM PAGE 21

closing with the Marines, and, as day approached, the fire slackened and died. For all the sound and fury, there were but six American casualties: two Marines dead, three others wounded; and the assistant surgeon, Dr. John B. Gibbs of the Navy, fatally shot through a lung. "He was dying hard," said Crane. "Hard. He was long past groaning. There was only the bitter strife for air which pulsed out into the night in a clear, penetrating whistle with intervals of terrible silence in which I held my own breath in the common unconscious aspiration to help. . ."

On the two succeeding nights it was the same. Again, in Huntington's words, the same "persistent and trifling attacks" out of the rocky, cactus-lined gullies, murdering sleep and burning up ammunition.

These attacks on the camp proved its location to be greatly exposed to enemy approaches through the thick brush. Consequently Huntington moved the camp toward lower ground, and the hill was made the main defensive position. But there was another problem: Commander Reiter, out in the bay aboard the *Panther*, found that his ship rode poorly after the Marines' equipment was unloaded. Thereupon he had the reserves of rifle ammunition judiciously distributed below as ballast, a measure which greatly increased his comfort. When Colonel Huntington sent for more ammunition, word came back that it was needed for ballast, and besides, if the Marines wanted any of their gear, they had better send working parties back to the ship to unload it. When Commander McCalla heard what Reiter had done, he sent off a sizzling order calculated to endear him to any Marine:

Sir: Break out immediately and land with the crew of the *Panther* 50,000 rounds of 6mm ammunition.

In future do not require Colonel Huntington to break out or land his stores or ammunition with members of his command.

Use your own officers and crew for this purpose and supply the commanding officer of Marines promptly with anything he may require.

Very soon afterward, Colonel Huntington named his new outpost Camp McCalla. Nothing was named for Reiter.

Manifestly, if Guantanamo Bay were to become a true "harbor of rest," there would have to be a showdown with the Spaniards at Cuzco. To drive them out and destroy their well became the day's business soon after reveille on June 14. With fifty Cuban scouts under Lieutenant Colonel Tomas to guide and flank the advance, Companies C and D of the Marine battalion were to move south, skirting the base of the hills, then east along the coral cliffs facing the Caribbean until Cuzco came in sight. While the two companies, led by Captain G. F. Elliott, followed their circuitous approach, a platoon under Lieutenant Louis J. Magill would strike out southward, across the mountains, so as to hit the Spaniards from inland and be in position to cut their line of retreat. From the seaward side the gunboat *Dolphin* would steam out of the bay and lie off Cuzco's open-ended valley, prepared to support the Marines once battle was joined.

An hour before noon the trap was set. Elliott's column worked its way into position, and Magill was virtually across the mountains. Then, with one gaunt, razor-backed ridge still remaining between the Marines and Cuzco Valley, a Spanish outpost caught sight of the attackers. Men of both sides raced pell-mell through the thornbushes and cactus to reach the top of the ridge. With the fifty-two-year-old Elliott in the lead, a platoon of Marines got there first, flung themselves out along the crest, and commenced firing down into the Spaniards.

Down in the valley, from the cover of thickets of sea-grape trees, the Spaniards fired back as best they could. Then Magill's platoon toiled up, caution forgotten, winded but full of fight. From the crest of another dominating ridge on Elliott's left, at the very inland end of the horseshoe-shaped valley, Magill joined the battle. At this moment, the *Dolphin*'s guns, pointing straight across Elliott's front and into Magill's line, began to shell the green clusters of sea grape, and four-inch "overs" whistled up among Magill's Marines with a crack and a clump that drove them to ground.

To check the deadly naval gunfire, there was only one expedient. Choosing a spot on the crest line, where every Spanish rifleman could see him, but also where the *Dolphin*'s gun-pointers could not mistake the signal, Sergeant John H. Quick improvised a semaphore flag out of a stick and a large bandanna, stood very straight—he was a tall, slim man—and commenced signaling the gunboat in Navy wigwag. Under a hail of rifle fire from less than two hundred yards away and with the *Dolphin*'s shell fragments whistling about him, Quick completed his message, punctiliously got it receipted for by the Navy signalman on the opposite end, and dropped to the ground unscratched, not knowing that he had just won a Medal of Honor. "I watched his face," Crane afterward wrote,

and it was as grave and serene as a man writing in his own library . . . I saw Quick betray only one sign of emotion. As he swung his clumsy flag to and fro, an end of it once caught on a cactus pillar, and he looked over his shoulder to see what had it. He gave the flag an impatient jerk. He looked annoyed.

Caught in the cross fire from the Marines and flayed by the gunboat's corrected shelling, the Spaniards began to give way, exposing themselves as they broke cover from among the sea grapes. At each open patch in the brush their dirty white uniforms, ill-suited for field service in Oriente, showed up as targets for the Marine riflemen, who, in Captain Elliott's words, "fired as coolly as at target practice." To harry the retreating enemy, Elliott sent on Tomas' guerrillas, who darted forward to complete the disorganization while the Marines mopped up Cuzco Valley, filled in the well, burned the Spanish *comandancia,* and took over a heliograph with which the Cuzco detachment had been reporting doings at Guantanamo Bay to General Pareja. One officer and seventeen Spanish enlisted men, some wounded, were captured; sixty more Spaniards were killed; and 150 others were reportedly wounded— all this at the cost of two Cubans killed and three Marines and two Cubans wounded (one the victim of an unintended discharge of Colonel Laborde's pistol at the height of battle). Heat stroke felled many more Americans than Spanish Mausers did.

The fight at the Cuzco well, the first pitched battle between American and Spanish troops during the war with Spain, ended the little campaign. The beaten Spaniards made their circuitous way back to their garrison in Guantanamo town, and although there were one or two minor guerrilla attacks on Marine outposts around Camp McCalla during succeeding months, no further real fighting took place ashore. To underscore the Marines' victory, Admiral Sampson sent the battleship *Texas* along from Santiago to bombard the fort at Cayo Toro on June 16, an action in which Commander McCalla and the *Marblehead* joined with gusto.

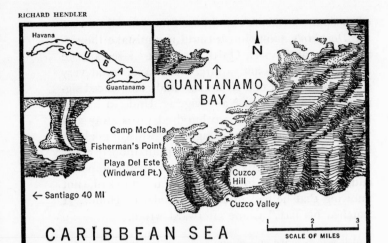

Havana

C U B A

Guantanamo

GUANTANAMO
BAY

N

Camp McCalla
Fisherman's Point
Playa Del Este
(Windward Pt.)

Cuzco
Hill

← Santiago 40 MI

Cuzco Valley

CARIBBEAN SEA

1 2 3
SCALE OF MILES

To wipe out the main Spanish position in Cuzco Valley, two companies of Marines marched south and east along the coast to occupy high ground to the west of the valley, while a platoon struck across the mountains from Camp McCalla to take the crest at its head. Their accurate rifle fire—and shelling from the seaward side by the Dolphin—*carried the day.*

Despite Lord Nelson's gloomy dictum, "A ship's a fool to fight a fort," the Navy had all the best of it in an hour's shelling that ended with all Spanish guns dismounted and the barracks in ruins.

In markedly edifying contrast to the ghastly casualties suffered from all forms of disease by the U.S. Army, only forty miles away at Santiago, the Marines had a negligible sick list. The reaction at home to the efficient operation at Guantanamo was one of immediate enthusiasm, which was only whetted as the scandals at nearby Santiago began to be known. Within less than a year, Congress tripled the permanent size of the Corps.

Throughout Shafter's bungled and malodorous campaign against Santiago, Guantanamo Bay served as the Navy's advance base, often harboring as many as a dozen ships for coaling or repairs. The *Vulcan,* first mobile repair ship in the Navy, accomplished sixty-three major jobs there. When the decision was made to capture Puerto Rico in July, 1898, Guantanamo was the rendezvous from which General Miles' expedition departed. Fully as important, the presence of United States troops ashore at Guantanamo pinned down Pareja's 7,000 men to guard the rear approaches of Santiago against an overland attack. Conceivably, in addition to providing the Navy with a superb base, the relatively small Guantanamo Bay campaign may have tipped larger scales at Santiago.

After hostilities ceased in August, 1898 (just as Colonel Huntington's Marines were poised to seize the port of Manzanillo, on the south coast of Cuba), the Navy continued to use Guantanamo as an anchorage. But the original cordiality between the Americans and the Cubans had dampened. Garcia, who had warmly welcomed the Navy and Marines at Guantanamo, had been mortally insulted at Santiago by General Shafter. The gouty 300-pound American general had declined to let Garcia or his men take part under arms in the final surrender of the Spanish. As for using the Cuban irregulars, whom Colonel Huntington had found "excellent . . . and fearless," Shafter thought they would best be employed as laborers about the army camps.

In the nature of things, and however necessary it was, the American occupation galled the Cubans. Had they been freed from Spain only to take on a new master? Màximo Gòmez, the Cuban generalissimo, had suspected American intentions all along, and it was useless to explain why Americans must establish at least some rudimentary governmental machine in Cuba. Racked by disease, malnutrition, ignorance, and Spanish cruelty (slavery had not been abolished in Cuba until the 1880's), Cubans had no experience at all of self-government. The tension increased, yet the Guantanamo area suffered less from the unrest and frustration with which the Cubans awaited the end of the American occupation: the Navy's hand was light, its garrison small.

In February, 1903, when Cuba's new government had attained independence, an agreement was reached between Theodore Roosevelt and Cuban President Tomás Estrada Palma, leasing to the United States in perpetuity, for $2,000 a year in gold, Guantanamo and another site, Bahia Honda, which was abandoned nine years later. (It lies just fifty miles west of Havana on the north coast of Cuba, facing Florida!)

In the spring of 1903, a congressional investigating party visited Guantanamo, and back in Washington appropriated $100,000 to set up the Guantanamo naval base; a joint Cuban-American commission, sitting aboard the U.S.S. *Olympia,* Dewey's flagship at Manila, laid out the exact boundaries of the U.S. reservation; the Navy formally took over on December 10, 1903.

From a strategic point of view, the new acquisition was very useful. With the completion of the Panama Canal it became more so. For Guantanamo Bay flanks the Windward Passage, through which sails more than half the Atlantic traffic entering and leaving the Caribbean. Yet for all its potential, which would not be realized until World War II, Guantanamo Bay remained for years little more than "a pile of coal" at the old coaling station on Hospital Cay. Each winter, when the fleet came south for maneuvers, the somnolent station, manned only by some 300 officers and men, would come to life for a few weeks, and the bay, normally almost empty, would then be serried by lines of battleships and cruisers. If there was trouble in Cuba —and generally there was, with three major revolutions between 1906 and 1918—an expeditionary force of Marines might be held in readiness under canvas on Deer Point, Guantanamo's springboard for West Indian and Caribbean interventions. Marines from the Deer Point camp went to Mexico in 1914, to Haiti in 1915, and to Santo Domingo in 1916; they were in and out of Cuba as governments rose and fell. Throughout World War I, a Marine brigade lay at "Gitmo," the Navy's nickname for the place, ready for action should the Germans seek to foment trouble at our back door.

In the lean years between world wars the base consisted of its dwindling coal pile (the last ship coaled at Guantanamo in 1937), a radio station, marine railways, and a cluster of tin-roofed green shops. As seen in 1926 by a correspondent of the *American Mercury*, life at Guantanamo had overtones of Kipling:

Here and there, a handful of officers, bleached as white as their uniforms under their wide pith helmets, plod doggedly along at their duties. If the day is not too hot, their wives are riding lazy ponies over the hill to call on the ladies of the Marine Corps at Deer Point. Chinese coolies methodically tend the boilers of the power plant or push tiny flat cars under the somnolent direction of a brown Cuban foreman . . . There is just enough tennis to keep in condition, just enough swimming to keep moderately cool, just enough bridge of an evening to exhaust the conversation . . .

But Guantanamo in those days contributed much, indirectly, to the morale of the U.S. Navy. It was the only place regularly visited by most of the Atlantic Fleet where a man could get a drink. To officers and men in the fell clutch of Prohibition, liberty runs up to Caimanera and Red Barn (just outside the station boundary) were a thirst-quenching treat.

Then, as the shadows began to fall over Europe, Guantanamo came to life. The Atlantic Fleet was strengthened. The Marines held landing exercises in the Caribbean almost every year from 1935 on. With stepped-up training and a larger Navy, and with worrisome speculations as to what Hitler's submarines might do to merchant shipping in the Caribbean, Guantanamo loomed larger. After France fell in 1940, a $5,000,000 contract was let for development of the naval station (before World War II ended, $34,000,000 would be spent). A reinforced Marine garrison worked night and day to install coastal batteries and antiaircraft positions; a radar rig, one of our very first, topped Paul Jones Hill overlooking Cuzco Valley.

On the day the Japanese attacked Pearl Harbor, Guantanamo had two airfields, a tank farm for fuel oil, a hospital, shops to support the fleet, and barracks for thousands of seamen and Marines. And the bay was never empty. After the German submarines struck (they were to sink 278 Allied ships in the Caribbean between December, 1941, and July, 1943), Guantanamo became a focal point in antisubmarine and convoy operations. As the Navy gradually won the submarine war, action slackened but training forged ahead. Before the war's end, more than two hundred warships got final "shakedown" training at Guantanamo.

Although there was a momentary lag in Guantanamo's pace after V-J Day, it picked up again under the demands of the cold war and the ceaseless training requirements of a thousand-ship Navy. In today's intense search for effective defense against hostile submarines, the underwater environment and configurations of Guantanamo's neighboring waters have proven ideal for training. In terms of modern strategic and logistic requirements (omitting its psychological importance), Guantanamo is a highly valuable staging and concentration point; and, for general war with a Communist enemy possessing perhaps 400 submarines, it could be the capstone of our defense of the Caribbean and the approaches to the Panama Canal.

Today, an airfield has leveled off most of McCalla Hill. Cuzco Valley is the site of a beach and recreation area. Farther up the valley, not far from the site of the Spanish *comandancia* which the Marines burned, lies a Navy cemetery. The mountain ridge that loomed behind Huntington's camp has borne the name Stephen Crane Hill for more than half a century, and Cayo Toro, once garrisoned by the Spanish, is inhabited only by land crabs and scorpions. Generations of Cubans, some descended from Laborde, Tomas, and Garcia, have grown up beside the naval base, have worked there, and have shared the prosperity it brought to the region. United States Marines still guard the base their forebears captured, and American warships still use the great bay for "a harbor of rest."

Until the advent of Castro's revolution, our tranquil tenancy of sunbaked Guantanamo was taken for granted as a symbol of common interests between Cuba and the United States. Since then, while loudly attacking our presence at Guantanamo and persistently harassing the base, the Cuban Communists have so far stopped short of that ultimate provocation which might justify reprisal. If Huntington and McCalla, long in their graves, could hear Fidel Castro's threats and his ranting over American occupancy of the bay which Cubans and Americans joined to wrest from Spain, they would be dumfounded. The Cubans were their friends.

Colonel Robert Debs Heinl, Jr., who now commands the Marines in Haiti, is a regular Marine officer, a veteran of Pearl Harbor, the South Pacific, Iwo Jima, and Korea. A contributor to the Encyclopaedia Britannica, The National Geographic, *and professional journals, he has just completed a new history of the Marine Corps,* Soldiers of the Sea (*U.S. Naval Institute, Annapolis, Maryland*).

CONTINUED FROM PAGE 17

wheel gave trouble because of shrinkage in the dry air of the desert, but then wedges could be driven under the tire. Eventually the tire might have to be taken off, heated red-hot, and reset on the wheel.

Although we are not well informed as to the exact dimensions of most parts of the wagon, for one wheel at least there is a meticulous measurement, made by William Clayton, a Mormon of the 1847 migration. Having decided to make an odometer, he carefully measured a hind wheel, and found it to be fourteen feet, eight inches in circumference, or four feet, eight inches in height. This was undoubtedly a large wheel; the average one probably stood almost a foot lower.

Front wheels were always smaller than hind wheels, to make the vehicle more maneuverable. On many wagons they were not more than six inches lower, preventing turns exceeding about thirty degrees. An occasional one had wheels so low that they would pass under the bed, and thus permit turns of ninety degrees or more, but small wheels made for harder pulling.

The ordinary wagon had neither springs nor brakes, but an essential part of the equipment was the "tar bucket." Traditionally it hung from the rear axle but was carried elsewhere when fording streams or traversing rocky passages. The term "tar" must be taken as highly flexible. Often the bucket contained tar or resin mixed half-and-half with tallow. Since these contents were used steadily to grease the wheels and kingbolt, the supply decreased, and before the end of the journey the emigrants might be using anything that came handy and would serve. A Mormon in '47 shot a wolf, apparently for mere rifle practice. He found the animal to be exceptionally fat, so he tried the fat out and added wolf grease to the mixture in the bucket. Later these same Mormons found an oil seep, and filled their buckets at it—thus being among the first Americans to use a petroleum lubricant.*

Such was the wagon in which the average pioneer rode to Oregon or California. And since his comfort —and sometimes his very life—depended on it, a man had an appreciation for a good one. The youthful Isaac Jones Wistar, later a Union general, started for California early in '49. On the street in Cincinnati a wagon caught his eye, and he sized it up as he might

*The Mexican *carreta*, by contrast, was never greased—a lack which Americans considered shiftless—and its screeching was notorious. An interesting etymological question is thus raised. Why, except by the ancient principle of *lucus a non lucendo*, should not the Americans, who were so fond of lubricant, (instead of the Mexicans, who never touched the stuff) be called *greasers*?

a horse or a woman—"light, strong, short-coupled." Then and there, though the wagon was in use, he made an offer. Later, he was able to write proudly:

I made no mistake, for that wagon proved to be one of the only two of our entire outfit which survived the searching trials of the rocks and mountains, of alkali plains and desiccating deserts, and actually reached the Pacific Coast.

Granted, then, that the four-wheeled wagon was to be the vehicle of empire, how was it to be hauled? There were three possibilities—horses, mules, oxen.

Many modern representations to the contrary, the horse was really ruled out from the beginning. Though that noble animal could move faster than the ox and could pull more than the mule, he could not match the ability of either to endure the long haul, the constant work, and the insufficient food. To do his best work, a horse needed grain, and grain could not be transported. Every train, indeed, had its riding horses, and these often got through. They were not, however, worked as hard as the team animals, and being more valuable, were given special care.

Only in the later years of the trail, from 1850 onward, did horse teams begin to be fairly common. By this time the road was better established, and swifter-moving transport had its advantages: grain was sometimes carried along so that the animals could have proper feed, at least during the first few weeks. To give them their due, the horses seem to have stood up well enough then, when the journey was not so arduous.

As between the mule and the ox, however, there doubtless were endless arguments around the campfires, punctuated by tobacco juice spat into the embers.

"Mules move faster."

"Yes, but oxen can pull more."

"Oxen don't stampede so easy."

"Yes, but when they do, they run worse."

It could go on forever. Mules bogged down in mud, but could live on cottonwood bark. The Plains Indians would steal mules, but not oxen. Oxen, however, were more likely to get sore feet.

As a "mule man" we may cite William Johnston, who crossed in '49 under the pilotage of James Stewart, an old Santa Fe trader who loved mules and handled them expertly. As Johnston wrote, "Stewart's concern is always for the mules—he wastes no thought on the men." Thus coddled, the animals responded vigorously: "It was a noble sight to see those small, tough, earnest, honest Spanish mules, every nerve strained to the utmost, examples of obedience, and of duty performed under trying circumstances." As the result of Stewart's efficiency, the men could claim that theirs was the first wagon train to get to California that year—and the mules were still in good condition.

As an "ox man" we have Peter H. Burnett, of '43, later to be the first governor of the state of California. In his train were both oxen and mules, and he found the oxen "greatly superior." He narrated their virtues thus: "The ox is a most noble animal, patient, thrifty, durable, gentle, and easily driven, and does not run off. Those who come to this country will be in love with their oxen by the time they reach here."

The expression "dumb ox" is not found in diaries of the migration. Oxen seem to have been at least as intelligent as mules and much more so than most horses. They were individually named, and had personality. J. Q. Thornton, of '46, may be called to testify. He has left us the names and characters of the eight in his four yoke. There was Brady, who died at South Pass. Thornton called Star and Golden "unreliable," though perhaps they were just intelligent and strong-willed: they used to hide in the thickets at yoking-up time, and then look innocent when found. Thornton mentioned four others as being good enough and "tolerably honest"—Sam, John, Tom, and Nig. But his love was Dick, who was all that an ox ought to be and was labeled in one word: "faultless."

The long-continued case of *Mule v. Ox,* as J. S. Holliday points out in his doctoral dissertation, could never really be decided.

Numerically, however, the verdict was in favor of the ox. In 1850 a count at Fort Laramie showed 36,116 oxen passing through and only 7,548 mules—and the latter figure apparently included pack-train animals. Quite possibly the deciding factor was the expense. One price list of the period gives the cost of a mule as $75 and of an ox as $25. Though the prices varied from year to year, the ratio probably remained about the same. In the long run the use of oxen became so prevalent that "ox-team emigrant" became a generic term.

The number of oxen to the wagon varied considerably. Four—that is, two yoke—was the minimum. Three yoke was perhaps the average, but four was not uncommon; six yoke was probably the maximum that could be handled on the twisting mountain roads. The bigger teams could haul heavier loads, and the strain on the individual animal was less. On the other hand, the more animals, the more work to guard and care for them, and pasturage had to be found.

Generally some of the cattle—especially in trains that included children—were milch cows. These were usually just driven along, but sometimes were put under the yoke. Extra cattle were usually taken along as spares and for a supply of fresh meat, though some people thought that such a herd was more nuisance than it was worth. The total number of cattle was thus regularly about twice that of the men and women.

The fate of most of these faithful beasts was a sad one. Rare was the ox or cow that lived to a quiet and respected old age on the deep-grassed pastures of Oregon or California. Many of them were slaughtered on the trail for beef, and we can scarcely even imagine that the best-loved ones were spared the longest. There was little place for sentiment on the desert, and the ox that began to fail was undoubtedly the one to be butchered. Remembering, however, that the ancient Greeks sacrificed an ox only after ritual weeping for the death of "man's companion," we can believe that on Goose Creek or along the Humboldt there were sad thoughts in him who did the deed, and tears in women's eyes, and the wailing of children—and perhaps the beef did not sit well, even on a very empty stomach. Yet this was another virtue of the ox, that he could thus yield food. Of course, the mule also could be, and was, eaten—but always with prejudice.

To every ox slaughtered, however, a dozen or a score died of disease, of drinking alkali water, of Digger arrows, of thirst, or of slow starvation and overwork. Notations on dead oxen are a monotonous feature of the diaries. J. Goldsborough Bruff of '49, a great counter, kept busy during five days on the Rabbit Hole and Black Rock stretch in northwestern Nevada, where someone had left a posted notice on a bit of broken axle: *This is the place of destruction to team.* Bruff's total was 603 dead oxen.

Such mass catastrophe may not move us as much as the death of one known individual animal. We may quote James Mason's elegy of August 2, 1850, on Cassia Creek: "Here we lost old Sock. He died rather sudden. He was much lamented by the boys as he was our main Sanby [stand-by] at the start."

We should remember a little the faithful beasts that died. Sometimes they dropped under the yokes and were left lying. Often they were merely abandoned, standing, too weak to follow, left a prey to the wolves. Sometimes a kindly bullet finished the matter. Except for a little meat cut off for food, no one bothered with the carcasses; on some stretches they lay so thick that a blind man could have followed the trail by the stench. Then for a few years the skeletons lay dazzling white in the desert sun, pale white under the moon.

In reckoning the price of the land we might well be no less thoughtful of the animals than that kindhearted Lord, the God of heaven, when he spoke to Jonah of saving the men—and beasts—of Nineveh. Yes, in that reckoning of the price we might remember his final words: ". . . and also much cattle."

Thus, in the end, the covered wagon is to be considered a kind of double symbol—the wagon itself and the oxen that pulled it. With this equipment the epic movement was accomplished.

In 1841 came the first attempts—unsuccessful, in that the emigrants were forced to leave their wagons and proceed on horseback or muleback or afoot. In '42, the wagons got through to Oregon. In '43 came the great migration to Oregon, and Joe Walker made a gallant try for California, though in the end he had to leave the three wagons. At last in '44 Elisha Stevens broke the Sierra barrier and took wagons across what would one day be called Donner Pass.

Thus, the emigration first pointed toward Oregon, and the term Oregon Trail has stuck. But from '46 onward, California tended to steal the show. In '49 came the cataclysm of the Gold Rush, and for a few years anyone going to Oregon was a curiosity. Indeed, '50 was probably bigger than '49, and, according to some, '52 was the biggest of all. The migration died down somewhat in the later fifties, and Oregon began to get a better share again.

The "trail" it was called—seldom the "road." The distinction is significant. "Trail," an Americanism in this sense, meant a route of travel that had been established merely by use. "Road" was reserved for something that had been definitely laid out and constructed, as was Lander's Road from the Sweetwater River to Fort Hall.

In many places you can still see the trail, sometimes even follow it for miles. Across the prairies and through the sagebrush there was easy going. Even there, however, the trail never runs straight, but always slightly sinuously—where the oxen of the lead team adjusted their course to inequalities of ground or growth, and where the following thousands, over two decades and more, kept to the same trace.

The trail never follows the contours of a hill, because the wagons had a high center of gravity and tipped easily, and because the making of a "dugway" was too much work for the emigrants. But almost no steepness of ascent deflects the trail, because the teams could be doubled. Nor does a sharp downgrade: one, two, or all four wheels could be locked, or the wagons could even be let down by ropes snubbed around trees. Lakes and swampy places could be skirted. Smaller streams were forded as a matter of course, the difficulty of getting down the bank into the stream often being greater than crossing it. Larger streams, up to about four feet in depth, could also be forded. Across the deeper ones the wagon beds were raised upon blocks set upon the axle and bolster, an uplift of about a foot being considered safe. The few streams that were still deeper had to be ferried, either by improvising rafts of logs or by calking and floating the wagon beds.

To generalize about the conditions of the long trek is difficult. The teams plodded monotonously westward. Heat, dust, and mosquitoes! Quarrels, resulting from too-long association in the same company! But the emigrants (they were always "emigrants" and never "immigrants") remembered good times also—dancing on the prairie, singing around the campfire, exciting chases after buffalo, breathtaking first sights of the wonders of this new land: snow-covered peaks in July, boiling springs, mirages, ancient volcanic craters.

Some of the wagon people were both strong in body and exuberant in personality, and these traits shine through in their diaries like lamps burning steadily. Such a one was Thomas Turnbull of '52. Nothing downed his optimism and enthusiasm. It was always: "the best feed I mostly ever saw . . . plenty of wood here . . . the handsomest roads I ever saw . . . the best grass of every kind I ever saw in the United States . . . the best road I ever saw, as level as a plank." (But, to be sure, he could also go to superlatives in the opposite direction: "Mosquitoes the worst I ever saw.")

Another one was Lydia Waters of '55. Everything had equal zest for her—driving oxen, or herding the loose cattle, or presiding at a childbirth. She seems quite in character when comparing a wattled hut to a champagne basket. Again, when she crossed the Forty-Mile Desert, she did not write of hell. But on arriving at the Truckee River, she could put it thus: "If I ever saw Heaven, I saw it there." Naturally she was the one who could write in retrospect: "There were many things to laugh about."

Danger and death, like battles in a war, were always a nerve-gnawing possibility, but they occurred on very few days. From year to year, according to the conditions, the face of peril changed. The first trains had the hardest time because of sheer geographical ignorance and the necessity of breaking trail. Partly by skill and stamina, partly by good luck, they got through with remarkably few casualties. The greatest disaster, that of the Donner party, did not come until '46, and then as the result of human duplicity and fallibility, and an early winter. The Forty-niners followed a crowded trail; their cattle died from lack of pasturage.

In '49 and several subsequent years, cholera rode the wagons out onto the plains, and there came to be a string of graves along the trail. In the later fifties there were difficulties with white desperadoes; one group captured an entire train, and sent the people off westward on foot.

And, of course, there were the Indian troubles, which gave rise to the greatest myth of the trail. The wagon

The leader of an Indian hunting party tries to block passage of an emigrant train. A prudent "train boss" usually came to terms with a powerful Plains tribe. This drawing was done for Harper's Weekly in 1874 by William de la Montagne Cary.

train of fiction—in Hough's *Covered Wagon,* for instance—moves from one desperate Indian attack to another. The record, however, shows little of this sort. The trains actually moved only by favor and friendship of the powerful Plains tribes.

A moment's reflection should show that this must be true. When the Sioux, Cheyenne, and Arapaho really went to war in the sixties, they fought and sometimes defeated whole armies. What would they have done with a few emigrants?

The wagon trains seem to have interested and amused the Indians. (Doubtless, life in the tepee became monotonous at times.) Besides, the emigrants could be cajoled or scared into giving gifts, which the Indians probably considered a kind of tribute. The emigrants had much more trouble with the despised Diggers in the desert country than they ever had with the lordly Sioux. For one reason, the emigrants themselves were on their good behavior among the powerful tribes. No one in his right mind went about insulting or mistreating a Sioux in the land of his own strength. But in '45 a half-breed emigrant wantonly shot a Paiute. Probably there were also unrecorded atrocities, and from that time on there was trouble along the Humboldt. In '46 something of a pitched battle occurred, and one white man was killed. Emigrants learned not to camp within bowshot of the willows that fringed any stream. Otherwise they might wake up to find several oxen crippled by arrows, and perhaps the cattle guard himself laid out, agape at the morning sun. The emigrants were likely to retaliate by shooting on sight.

But all this is very different from the epic legend of the beleaguered wagon train. We all know the picture: the wagons are drawn up in a circle; from them the men fire their rifles; around the outside the mounted Indians circle on their horses, shooting with their bows.

How often did it happen? I have been reading covered-wagon records for a long time now. All I can say is that I have never found *one* such example.

We can see why, if we consider the realities. The Plains Indian was a good fighter, but he had no more liking than any other man for getting himself killed. Once a wagon train was in position, garrisoned by some determined riflemen, all the odds were against the Indian. The bullets far outranged his arrows, and he and his pony would have had little chance of even getting within bowshot of the enemy before being brought down. Why should any professional warrior thus gallop around and let himself be shot at? Why—especially when he could just as well wait until the wagon train was strung out helplessly on the trail? The beleaguered wagon train is one part of the story which I think we shall have to give over to the writers of fiction.

Otherwise, I can see no reason to start debunking the covered-wagon story. It might even be built up a little. Its very audacity—an attempt to cross two thousand miles of wilderness—is breathtaking. Those who love to sing the praises of free enterprise should make

more of it. Here was free enterprise at its rawest. Until the later fifties, the travelers got no appreciable government aid, not even for exploration. Except for the Mormons, there is nothing that can be called large-scale corporate action. The unit was the family.

In this last connection we come to another source of continuing interest in the story. The frontier, in most of its dramatic history, is a man's world. Exploration, trapping, Indian fighting—here the women and children had no place except by accident. Even in the mining camp and on the cattle ranch, women were so scarce that the novelist usually had to go to great trouble to import a schoolmarm or someone's far-strayed daughter. But the families were right there in the covered wagons—the women and children often outnumbering the men. And family life kept right on. If there was a preacher along, like the Reverend Mr. Dunleavy in '46, he was likely to be called upon not only for funerals but also for marriages. From the number of children born less than nine months after the arrival of the trains in Oregon or California, we should judge that the amenities of family life were not neglected during the journey. On the other hand, pregnancy was no bar against setting out. The Stevens party of '44 arrived stronger by two than when it left. Even that first migration, of '41, had a woman along. This was Mrs. Nancy Kelsey, a ripe eighteen years of age, who stated roundly, "Where my husband goes, I can go," and went—taking a baby with her. So did others—the women following their men, the children with them.

The graves of all three lined the trail. In the early years the herd was milled over a new-made grave or the wagons run across it, so that the Indians could not find it and dig the body up. In later years, when there were more emigrants and few Indians, little headboards or crosses of wood stood along the trail. But certainly we should not accept that slogan, "The weak died by the way." Since when did Death refuse to take the strong? They may go to him first by their very strength. So, sometimes, we think, reading the words that the keepers of the diaries copied down.

M. De Morst, of Col: Ohio,
died Sep. 16th. 1849
Aged 50 years, Of Camp Fever.

Jno A. Dawson, St. Louis, Mo.
Died Oct. 1st, 1849
from eating a poisonous root at the spring.

Mr. Eastman;—
The deceased was killed by
an Indian arrow; Octr. 4th, 1849

Saml. A. Fitzzimmons, died from
effects of a wound received from a
bowie-knife in the hands of Geo. Symington
Aug. 25th 1849

Died: "Of cholera . . . Of cholera . . . Of cholera." (That most often!) *Died:* "Of accidental discharge of his gun." *Died:* (there was a doctor in this company) "Disease, Gastro Enterites Typhoid." *Died:* "Of drowning." Often, simply: "Died."

Died: "From Southport, Wisconsin . . . Late of Galena, Ill. . . . Of Selma, Alabama . . . From Yorkshire, England . . . Of Buffalo, N.Y." *Died:* sometimes with only the name for identification.

Died: "Mrs. Mildred Moss, wife of D. H. T. Moss." *Died* (as if registering in some last hotel): "Robert Gilmore and wife." *Died:* "Frederic William, son of James M. and Mary Fulkerson." *Died* (two weeks farther westward): "Mary, consort of J. M. Fulkerson."

Died: "Mrs. Emmaline Barnes, Amanda and Mahela Robbins, three sisters in one grave, Indiana."

There were graves without names: "The remains of a dead man dug up by wolves, and reburied."

Some were laid in their graves succinctly, perhaps as time pressed; some were granted a few more words:

Samuel McFarlin, of Wright Co Mo. died
27th Sep. 1849, of fever, Aged, 44 years.—
*May he rest peaceably in this
savage unknown country*

Jno. Hoover, died, June 18. 49
Aged 12 yrs. Rest in peace,
sweet boy, for thy travels are over.

As Virgil wrote: *Tantae molis erat Romanam condere gentem.* Yes, it was a great labor to establish the Roman people. So also it was to pass the barrier of mountains and deserts and thus round out the shape of a republic. The covered wagon stands as the symbol, and we should not forget its dead. "All this too was part of the price of the taking-over of the land."

George R. Stewart, professor of English at the University of California, Berkeley, is the author of the well-known novels, Storm *and* Fire, *as well as of a number of nonfictional works. His long-standing interest in the American West has been demonstrated in such books as* Ordeal by Hunger, The Story of the Donner Party. *McGraw-Hill will soon publish his history of the California Trail.*

For further reading: The Year of Decision, 1846 *(Little, Brown, 1942) and* Across the Wide Missouri *(Houghton Mifflin, 1947), both by Bernard De Voto;* The Overland Trail, *by Jay Monaghan (Bobbs-Merrill, 1947);* The Far Western Frontier, *by Ray Allen Billington (Harper & Brothers, 1956).*

Middle Passage

CONTINUED FROM PAGE 25

Long, the Jamaica planter and historian, justified the cruel punishments inflicted on slaves by saying, "The many acts of violence they have committed by murdering whole crews and destroying ships when they had it in their power to do so have made these rigors wholly chargeable on their own bloody and malicious disposition which calls for the same confinement as if they were wolves or wild boars." For "wolves or wild boars" a modern reader might substitute "men who would rather die than be enslaved."

With the loading of the slaves, the captain, for his part, had finished what he regarded as the most difficult part of his voyage. Now he had to face only the ordinary perils of the sea, most of which were covered by his owners' insurance against fire, shipwreck, pirates and rovers, letters of mart and counter-mart, barratry, jettison, and foreign men-of-war. Among the risks not covered by insurance, the greatest was that of the cargo's being swept away by disease. The underwriters refused to issue such policies, arguing that they would expose the captain to an unholy temptation. If insured against disease among his slaves, he might take no precautions against it and might try to make his profit out of the insurance.

The more days at sea, the more deaths among his cargo, and so the captain tried to cut short the next leg of his voyage. If he had shipped his slaves at Bonny, Old Calabar, or any port to the southward, he might call at one of the Portuguese islands in the Gulf of Guinea for an additional supply of food and fresh water, usually enough, with what he had already, to last for three months. If he had traded to the northward, he made straight for the West Indies. Usually he had from four to five thousand nautical miles to sail—or even more, if the passage was from Angola to Virginia. The shortest passage—that from the Gambia River to Barbados—might be made in as little as three weeks, with favoring winds. If the course was much longer, and if the ship was becalmed in the doldrums or driven back by storms, it might take more than three months to cross the Atlantic, and slaves and sailors would be put on short rations long before the end of the Middle Passage.

On a canvas of heroic size, Thomas Stothard, Esquire, of the Royal Academy, depicted *The Voyage of the Sable Venus from Angola to the West In-dies*. His painting (see page 24) is handsomely reproduced in the second volume of Bryan Edwards' *History of the British Colonies in the West Indies* (1793), where it appears beside a poem on the same allegorical subject by an unnamed Jamaican author, perhaps Edwards himself.

The joint message of the poem and the painting is simple to the point of coarseness: that slave women are preferable to English girls at night, being passionate and accessible; but the message is embellished with classical details, to show the painter's learning.

Meanwhile the Sable Venus, if she was a living woman carried from Angola to the West Indies, was roaming the deck of a ship that stank of excrement; as was said of any slaver, "You could smell it five miles down wind." She had been torn from her husband and her children, she had been branded on the left buttock, and she had been carried to the ship bound hand and foot, lying in the bilge at the bottom of a dugout canoe. Now she was the prey of the ship's officers.

Here is how she and her shipmates spent the day.

If the weather was clear, they were brought on deck at eight o'clock in the morning. The men were attached by their leg irons to the great chain that ran along the bulwarks on both sides of the ship; the women and half-grown boys were allowed to wander at will. About nine o'clock the slaves were served their first meal of the day. If they were from the Windward Coast—roughly, the shoreline of present-day Liberia and Sierra Leone—the fare was boiled rice, millet, or corn meal, sometimes cooked with a few lumps of salt beef abstracted from the sailors' rations. If they were from the Bight of Biafra, at the east end of the Gulf of Guinea, they were fed stewed yams, but the Congos and the Angolas preferred manioc or plantains. With the food they were all given half a pint of water, served out in a pannikin.

After the morning meal came a joyless ceremony called "dancing the slaves." "Those who were in irons," says Dr. Thomas Trotter, surgeon of the *Brookes* in 1783, "were ordered to stand up and make what motions they could, leaving a passage for such as were out of irons to dance around the deck." Dancing was prescribed as a therapeutic measure, a specific against suicidal melancholy, and also against scurvy—although in the latter case it was a useless torture for men with swollen limbs. While sailors paraded the deck, each with a cat-o'-nine-tails in his right hand, the men slaves "jumped in their irons" until their ankles were bleeding flesh. Music was provided by a slave thumping on a broken drum or an upturned kettle, or by an African banjo, if there was one aboard, or perhaps by a sailor with a bagpipe or a fiddle. Slaving captains sometimes advertised for "A person that can play on the Bagpipes, for a Guinea ship." The slaves were also told to sing. Said Dr. Claxton after his voyage in the *Young Hero,* "They sing, but not for their amusement. The captain ordered them to sing, and they sang songs of sorrow. Their sickness, fear of being beaten, their hunger, and the memory of their country, etc., are the usual subjects."

While some of the sailors were dancing the slaves, others were sent below to scrape and swab out the sleeping rooms. It was a sickening task, and it was not well performed unless the captain imposed an iron discipline. James Barbot, Sr., was proud of the discipline maintained on the *Albion-Frigate.* "We were very nice," he says, "in keeping the places where the slaves lay clean and neat, appointing some of the ship's crew to do that office constantly and thrice a week we perfumed betwixt decks with a quantity of good vinegar in pails, and red-hot iron bullets in them, to expel the bad air, after the place had been well washed and scrubbed with brooms." Captain Hugh Crow, the last legal English slaver, was famous for his housekeeping. "I always took great pains," he says, "to promote the health and comfort of all on board, by proper diet, regularity, exercise, and cleanliness, for I considered that on keeping the ship clean and orderly, which was always my hobby, the success of our voyage mainly depended." Certainly he lost fewer slaves in the Middle Passage than the other captains, some of whom had the filth in the hold cleaned out only once a week.

At three or four in the afternoon the slaves were fed their second meal, often a repetition of the first. Sometimes, instead of African food, they were given horse beans, the cheapest provender from Europe. The beans were boiled to a pulp, then covered with a mixture of palm oil, flour, water, and red pepper, which the sailors called "slabber sauce." Most of the slaves detested horse beans, especially if they were used to eating yams or manioc. Instead of eating the pulp, they would, unless carefully watched, pick it up by handfuls and throw it in each other's faces.

That second meal was the end of their day. As soon as it was finished they were sent below, under the guard of sailors charged with stowing them away on their bare floors and platforms. The tallest men were placed amidships, where the vessel was widest; the shorter ones were tumbled into the stern. Usually there was only room for them to sleep on their sides, "spoon fashion." Captain William Littleton told Parliament that slaves in the ships on which he sailed might lie on their backs if they wished—"though perhaps," he conceded, "it might be difficult all at the same time."

After stowing their cargo, the sailors climbed out of the hatchway, each clutching his cat-o'-nine-tails; then the hatchway gratings were closed and barred. Sometimes in the night, as the sailors lay on deck and tried to sleep, they heard from below "an howling melancholy noise, expressive of extreme anguish." When Dr. Trotter told his interpreter, a slave woman, to inquire about the cause of the noise, "she discovered it to be owing to their having dreamt they were in their own country, and finding themselves when awake, in the hold of a slave ship."

More often the noise heard by the sailors was that of quarreling among the slaves. The usual occasion for quarrels was their problem of reaching the latrines. These were inadequate in size and number, and hard to find in the darkness of the crowded hold, especially by men who were ironed together in pairs.

In squalls or rainy weather, the slaves were never brought on deck. They were served their two meals in the hold, where the air became too thick and poisonous to breathe. Dr. Falconbridge writes:

For the purpose of admitting fresh air, most of the ships in the slave-trade are provided, between the decks, with five or six air-ports on each side of the ship, of about six inches in length and four in breadth; in addition to which, some few ships, but not one in twenty, have what they denominate wind-sails [funnels made of canvas and so placed as to direct a current of air into the hold]. But whenever the sea is rough and the rain heavy, it becomes necessary to shut these and every other conveyance by which the air is admitted. . . . The negroes' rooms very soon become intolerably hot. The

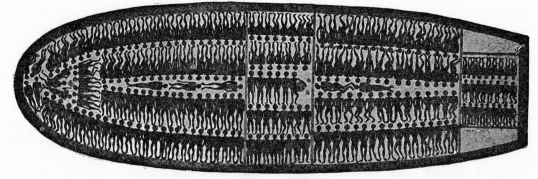

As this diagram shows, grasping owners utilized every square foot of a slave ship's lower decks.

confined air, rendered noxious by the effluvia exhaled from their bodies and by being repeatedly breathed, soon produces fevers and fluxes which generally carry off great numbers of them.

Dr. Trotter says that when tarpaulins were thrown over the gratings, the slaves would cry, "Kickeraboo, kickeraboo, we are dying, we are dying." Falconbridge gives one instance of their sufferings:

Some wet and blowing weather having occasioned the portholes to be shut and the grating to be covered, fluxes and fevers among the negroes ensued. While they were in this situation, I frequently went down among them till at length their rooms became so extremely hot as to be only bearable for a very short time. But the excessive heat was not the only thing that rendered their situation intolerable. The deck, that is, the floor of their rooms, was so covered with the blood and mucus which had proceeded from them in consequence of the flux, that it resembled a slaughter-house.

While the slaves were on deck they had to be watched at all times to keep them from committing suicide. Says Captain Phillips of the *Hannibal*, "We had about 12 negroes did wilfully drown themselves, and others starv'd themselves to death; for," he explained, "'tis their belief that when they die they return home to their own country and friends again."

This belief was reported from various regions, at various periods of the trade, but it seems to have been especially strong among the Ibos of eastern Nigeria. In 1788, nearly a hundred years after the *Hannibal*'s voyage, Dr. Ecroide Claxton was the surgeon who attended a shipload of Ibos. Some, he testified,

wished to die on an idea that they should then get back to their own country. The captain in order to obviate this idea, thought of an expedient viz. to cut off the heads of those who died intimating to them that if determined to go, they must return without heads. The slaves were accordingly brought up to witness the operation. One of them by a violent exertion got loose and flying to the place where the nettings had been unloosed in order to empty the tubs, he darted overboard. The ship brought to, a man was placed in the main chains to catch him which he perceiving, made signs which words cannot express expressive of his happinesss in escaping. He then went down and was seen no more.

Dr. Isaac Wilson, a surgeon in the Royal Navy, made a Guinea voyage on the *Elizabeth*, captain John Smith, who was said to be very humane. Nevertheless, Wilson was assigned the duty of flogging the slaves. "Even in the act of chastisement," Wilson says, "I have seen them look up at me with a smile, and, in their own language, say 'presently we shall be no more.'" One woman on the *Elizabeth* found some rope yarn, which she tied to the armorer's vise; she fastened the other end round her neck and was found dead in the morning. On the *Brookes* when Thomas Trotter was her sur-

geon, there was a man who, after being accused of witchcraft, had been sold into slavery with all his family. During the first night on shipboard he tried to cut his throat. Dr. Trotter sewed up the wound, but on the following night the man not only tore out the stitches but tried to cut his throat on the other side. From the ragged edges of the wound and the blood on his fingers, he seemed to have used his nails as the only available instrument. His hands were tied together after the second wound, but he refused all food, and he died of hunger in eight or ten days.

Besides the propensity for suicide, another deadly scourge of the Guinea cargoes was a phenomenon called "fixed melancholy." Even slaves who were well fed, treated with kindness, and kept under relatively sanitary conditions would often die, one after another, for no apparent reason; they had simply lost the will to live. Dr. Wilson believed that fixed melancholy was responsible for the loss of two thirds of the slaves who died on the *Elizabeth*. "No one who had it was ever cured," he says, "whereas those who had it not and yet were ill, recovered. The symptoms are a lowness of spirits and despondency. Hence they refuse food. This only increases the symptoms. The stomach afterwards got weak. Hence the belly ached, fluxes ensued, and they were carried off." But in spite of the real losses from despair, the high death rate on Guineamen was due to somatic more than to psychic afflictions.

Along with their human cargoes, crowded, filthy, undernourished, and terrified out of the wish to live, the ships also carried an invisible cargo of microbes, bacilli, spirochetes, viruses, and intestinal worms from one continent to another; the Middle Passage was a crossroad and market place of diseases. From Europe came smallpox, measles (somewhat less deadly to Africans than to American Indians), gonorrhea, and syphilis (which last Columbus' sailors had carried from America to Europe). The African diseases were yellow fever (to which the natives were resistant), dengue, blackwater fever, and malaria (which was not specifically African, but which most of the slaves carried in their blood streams). If anopheles mosquitoes were present, malaria spread from the slaves through any new territories to which they were carried. Other African diseases were amoebic and bacillary dysentery (known as "the bloody flux"), Guinea worms, hookworm (possibly African in origin, but soon endemic in the warmer parts of the New World), yaws, elephantiasis, and leprosy.

The particular affliction of the white sailors after escaping from the fevers of the Guinea Coast was scurvy, a deficiency disease to which they were exposed by their monotonous rations of salt beef and sea biscuits. The daily tot of lime juice (originally lemon juice) that prevented scurvy was almost never served on merchantmen during the days of the legal slave trade, and in fact was not prescribed in the Royal Navy until 1795. Although the slaves were also subject to scurvy, they fared better in this respect than the sailors, partly because they made only one leg of the triangular voyage and partly because their rough diet was sometimes richer in vitamins. But sailors and slaves alike were swept away by smallpox and "the bloody flux," and sometimes whole shiploads went blind from what seems to have been trachoma.

Smallpox was feared more than other diseases, since the surgeons had no way of curing it. One man with smallpox infected a whole vessel, unless—as sometimes happened—he was tossed overboard when the first scabs appeared. Captain Wilson of the *Briton* lost more than half his cargo of 375 slaves by not listening to his surgeon. It was the last slave on board who had the disease, says Henry Ellison, who made the voyage. "The doctor told Mr. Wilson it was the small-pox," Ellison continues. "He would not believe it, but said he would keep him, as he was a fine man. It soon broke out amongst the slaves. I have seen the platform one continued scab. We hauled up eight or ten slaves dead of a morning. The flesh and skin peeled off their wrists when taken hold of, being entirely mortified."

But dysentery, though not so much feared, probably caused more deaths in the aggregate. Ellison testified that he made two voyages on the *Nightingale*. On the first voyage the slaves were so crowded that thirty boys "messed and slept in the long boat all through the Middle Passage, there being no room below"; and still the vessel lost only five or six slaves in all, out of a cargo of 270. On the second voyage, however, the *Nightingale* buried "about 150, chiefly of fevers and flux. We had 250 when we left the coast."

The average mortality in the Middle Passage is impossible to state accurately from the surviving records. Some famous voyages were made without the loss of a single slave. On one group of nine voyages between 1766 and 1780, selected at random, the vessels carried 2,362 slaves and there were no epidemics of disease. The total loss of slaves was 154, or about six and one-half per cent. That figure is to be compared with the losses on a list of twenty voyages compiled by Thomas Clarkson, the abolitionist, in which the vessels carried 7,904 slaves with a mortality of 2,053, or twenty-six per cent. Balancing high and low figures together, the English Privy Council in 1789 arrived at an estimate of twelve and one-half per cent for the average mortality among slaves in the Middle Passage. To this figure it added four and one-half per cent for the deaths of slaves in harbors before they were sold, and thirty-three per cent for deaths in the so-called "seasoning" or acclima-

tizing process, making a total of fifty per cent. If these figures are correct, only one slave was added to the New World labor force for every two purchased on the Guinea Coast.

To keep the figures in perspective, it might be said that the mortality among slaves in the Middle Passage was possibly no greater than that of white indentured servants or even of free Irish, Scottish, and German immigrants in the North Atlantic crossing. On the better-commanded Guineamen it was probably less, and for a simple economic reason. There was no profit on a slaving voyage until the Negroes were landed alive and sold; therefore the better captains took care of their cargoes. It was different on the North Atlantic crossing, where even the hold and steerage passengers paid their fares before coming aboard, and where the captain cared little whether they lived or died.

After leaving the Portuguese island of São Tomé—if he had watered there—a slaving captain bore westward along the equator for a thousand miles, and then northwestward toward the Cape Verde Islands. This was the tedious part of the Middle Passage. "On leaving the Gulf of Guinea," says the author of a *Universal Geography* published in the early nineteenth century, ". . . that part of the ocean must be traversed, so fatal to navigators, where long calms detain the ships under a sky charged with electric clouds, pouring down by torrents of rain and of fire. This *sea of thunder,* being a focus of mortal diseases, is avoided as much as possible, both in approaching the coasts of Africa and those of America." It was not until reaching the latitude of the Cape Verde Islands that the vessel fell in with the northeast trades and was able to make a swift passage to the West Indies.

Dr. Claxton's ship, the *Young Hero,* was one of those delayed for weeks before reaching the trade winds. "We were so streightened for provisions," he testified, "that if we had been ten more days at sea, we must either have eaten the slaves that died, or have made the living slaves *walk the plank,*" a term, he explained, that was widely used by Guinea captains. There are no authenticated records of cannibalism in the Middle Passage, but there are many accounts of slaves killed for various reasons. English captains believed that French vessels carried poison in their medicine chests, "with which they can destroy their negroes in a calm, contagious sickness, or short provisions." They told the story of a Frenchman from Brest who had a long passage and had to poison his slaves; only twenty of them reached Haiti out of five hundred. Even the cruelest English captains regarded this practice as Latin, depraved, and uncovered by their insurance policies. In an emergency they simply jettisoned part of their cargo.

Often a slave ship came to grief in the last few days of the Middle Passage. It might be taken by a French privateer out of Martinique, or it might disappear in a tropical hurricane, or it might be wrecked on a shoal almost in sight of its harbor. On a few ships there was an epidemic of suicide at the last moment.

These, however, were exceptional disasters, recounted as horror stories in the newspapers of the time. Usually the last two or three days of the passage were a comparatively happy period. All the slaves, or all but a few, might be released from their irons. When there was a remaining stock of provisions, the slaves were given bigger meals—to fatten them for market—and as much water as they could drink. Sometimes on the last day—if the ship was commanded by an easy-going captain—there was a sort of costume party on deck, with the women slaves dancing in the sailors' castoff clothing. Then the captain was rowed ashore, to arrange for the disposition of his cargo.

This was a problem solved in various fashions. In Virginia, if the vessel was small, it might sail up and down the tidal rivers, bartering slaves for tobacco at private wharves. There were also public auctions of newly imported slaves, usually at Hampton, Yorktown, or Bermuda Hundred. In South Carolina, which was the great mainland slave market, the cargo was usually consigned to a commission merchant, who disposed of the slaves at auction, then had the vessel loaded with rice or indigo for its voyage back to England.

In the smaller West Indian islands, the captain sometimes took charge of selling his own slaves. In this case he ferried them ashore, had them drawn up in a ragged line of march, and paraded them through town with bagpipes playing, before exposing them to buyers in the public square. In the larger islands, commission merchants took charge of the cargo, and the usual method of selling the slaves at retail was a combination of the "scramble"—to be described in a moment—with the vendue or public auction "by inch of candle."

First the captain, with the commission merchant at his side, went over the cargo and picked out the slaves who were maimed or diseased. These were carried to a tavern and auctioned off, with a lighted candle before the auctioneer; bids were received until an inch of candle had burned. The price of so-called "refuse" slaves sold at auction was usually less than half of that paid for a healthy Negro. "I was informed by a mulatto woman," Dr. Falconbridge says, "that she purchased a sick slave at Grenada, upon speculation, for the small sum of one dollar, as the poor wretch was apparently dying of the flux." There were some slaves so diseased and emaciated that they could not be sold for even a dollar, and these might be left to die on the wharves without food or water.

The healthy slaves remaining after the auction were sold by "scramble," that is, at standard prices for each man, each woman, each boy, and each girl in the cargo. The prices were agreed upon with the purchasers, who then scrambled for their pick of the slaves. During his four voyages Falconbridge was present at a number of scrambles. "In the *Emilia*," he says,

at Jamaica, the ship was darkened with sails, and covered round. The men slaves were placed on the main deck, and the women on the quarter deck. The purchasers on shore were informed a gun would be fired when they were ready to open the sale. A great number of people came on board with tallies or cards in their hands, with their own names upon them, and rushed through the barricado door with the ferocity of brutes. Some had three or four handkerchiefs tied together, to encircle as many as they thought fit for their purposes.

For the slaves, many of whom believed that they were about to be eaten, it was the terrifying climax of a terrifying voyage.

The parliamentary investigations of 1788–1791 presented a complete picture of the Middle Passage, with testimony from everyone concerned except the slaves, and it horrified the English public. Powerful interests in Parliament, especially those representing the Liverpool merchants and the West Indian planters, prevented the passage of restrictive legislation at that time. But the Middle Passage was not forgotten, and in 1807 Parliament passed a law forbidding any slaver to sail from a British port after May 1 of that year. At about the same time, Congress prohibited the importation of slaves into American territory from and after January 1, 1808. All the countries of Europe followed the British and American example, if with some delay. During the next half century, however, reformers would learn that the trade was difficult to abolish in fact as well as in law, and that illegal slaving would continue as long as slavery itself was allowed to flourish.

One of America's best-known literary critics, Malcolm Cowley has long been interested in the history of slavery. Daniel P. Mannix, who collaborated with him on this article, is the author of a book on the slave trade which Viking Press will publish this spring.

The difficulties of abolishing the transoceanic slave trade are detailed in "Patrolling the Middle Passage" in the October, 1958, AMERICAN HERITAGE.

READING, WRITING, AND HISTORY

By BRUCE CATTON

At the Edge of Glory

One of the fascinating subchapters of history is the story of the man who did not quite make it—the talented man, richly deserving, who rises very near to the top and then, in a sudden moment of crisis, sees all that he has gained slip away from him. Looking back afterward we may see clearly that his solid achievements greatly outweigh his failures. Taken all in all, his career has been a success. Yet the real pinnacle eludes him, and instead of coming down in history as one of the country's giants, he is remembered simply as a good competent man who lacked something—good fortune, perhaps, or the capacity for doing precisely the right thing at a time of extreme pressure.

Sometimes, with such a man, a full reappraisal is called for. History can render faulty verdicts; now and then a man is fully entitled to a sort of posthu-

---

The Edge of Glory: A Biography of General William S. Rosecrans, U.S.A., by William H. Lamers. Harcourt, Brace & World, Inc. 499 pp. $6.95.

---

mous promotion. In other cases history's verdict seems fair enough, but we are left with the tantalizing realization of the part that luck can play in the life of a man or a nation.

The American Civil War is especially rich in cases of this sort, partly no doubt because it saw so many

obscure men placed in the center of the stage with incalculable values depending on their actions. Their contemporaries rendered judgment on them while the heat was still on; they looked for concrete results, and they did not always bother to make an objective examination of the way those results were achieved.

One of the most interesting of all the Civil War soldiers is William S. Rosecrans, major general in the United States Army, a solid soldier and also a man of genuine brilliance, who—if things had gone just a little differently—could conceivably have gone on to occupy the place U. S. Grant finally occupied. His story is examined in detail by William M. Lamers in a spirited biography, *The Edge of Glory*.

Rosecrans is worth knowing: a burly, red-faced man, jovial, well-liked by his soldiers, devoutly religious but gifted with a sure command of profane idiom, loyal to the Union, refusing to play politics—all in all, a good man. His military record was excellent. As McClellan's right-hand man he was largely responsible for McClellan's successful campaign in West Virginia in the first year of the war. He served with distinction under Grant, winning the battles of Iuka and Corinth and having a bitter falling-out with Grant afterward: these two battles fell just a little short of the sweeping success that both men wanted, and they argued over who was at fault. Rosecrans took over the dejected Army of the Cumberland after Don Carlos Buell was removed, restored its morale, and fought and won the Battle of Stones River at the end of 1862.

Lincoln went on record as considering the Stones River victory one of the most important of the war.

Actually, the battle was a stand-off; the Union army came within a hairsbreadth of rout, and was at last able to claim a win simply because the Confederate commander, the inexplicable Braxton Bragg, retreated from the field after having telegraphed to Richmond that he had won a great triumph. Yet however it may finally be judged, the battle did show Rosecrans as owning one of the basic traits of a great field commander—inability to admit that he had been licked.

In the following summer came Rosecrans' most glittering achievement: the campaign of maneuver which compelled Bragg to evacuate central Tennessee, including the vital city of Chattanooga, and retreat into northern Georgia. This was as fine a strategic accomplishment as any in the war, and it fully establishes Rosecrans' claim to high rank as a military leader. At the middle of September, 1863, the national administration might with justice have concluded that Rosecrans was its best general.

It never came to that conclusion, because this campaign, like Rosecrans' own rise, came to a full stop at Chickamauga.

When Bragg retreated, Rosecrans pursued, and in pursuit he was careless, apparently assuming that his only problem was to overtake the foe who was running away so fast. But Bragg was strongly reinforced, and he turned to strike, and Rosecrans had let his army get so scattered that Bragg might have regained all he had lost if he had recognized and used his opportunity promptly. In the end, Bragg gave Rosecrans just time enough to pull his army together, and when the Confederate blow was struck—on September 19 and 20—the Federal general had his men in hand.

Sometimes it seems that Chickamauga must have been one of the most completely dreadful of all Civil War battles. The two armies all but wrecked themselves. Each one lost approximately twenty-eight per cent of the total number on the field, the butcher's bill for the two armies together ran to an appalling 34,000, and the old legend which said that the word Chickamauga meant "river of blood" got abundant confirmation. And for Rosecrans personally, the battle was unmitigated disaster.

One of this general's troubles was that battle overstimulated him. He was the bravest of the brave, but in action he grew excitable, issuing too many orders too rapidly, acting sometimes on inadequate knowledge. It was so here. Toward noon on the second day, Rosecrans overhastily moved a division from a comparatively quiet sector to a place that was under heavy pressure. The movement left a temporary gap in the Federal line, and before the gap could be closed the hard-hitting General James Longstreet struck into it with an army corps. The whole right wing of Rosecrans' army was routed, and the General himself was caught up in the rout and separated from the main battlefield. Apparently the spark went out of him. For once in his life he admitted defeat. He rode back to Chattanooga, letting the rest of the battle fight itself. In the end he had to stand siege in Chattanooga, on the defensive, his bright prospects gone.

Mr. Lamers suggests that the defeat looked a great deal worse than it really was; that if Rosecrans had lost a battle he had nevertheless won the campaign, whose great objective had been to occupy and hold Chattanooga, and this led ultimately to the bisection of the Confederacy; and that because both Grant and Secretary of War Stanton disliked him, Rosecrans was relieved of his command when he ought to have been retained. His argument is persuasive, even if not wholly convincing: at the very least it makes it clear that there is a good deal to be said on the side of this general whose career was wrecked.

In any case, Rosecrans was shelved, then and thereafter, and his qualities all in all were good enough to entitle him to this reappraisal. He was one of those men who, as the title of the book suggests, touched the edge of glory without going any farther.

Rock of Chickamauga

The man who succeeded Rosecrans, of course, was General George H. Thomas, who saved the day at Chickamauga and was known as "The Rock" forever after; a man whose fame was immeasurably enhanced by the very defeat which put Rosecrans' own fame under an enduring cloud. Yet if Thomas won national acclaim for what he did at Chickamauga, he remains another general who, almost unaccountably, was somehow deprived of the full measure of recognition he might have had. His record contains no blots, yet he was obscured by others: the towering reputations of men like Grant, Sherman, and Sheridan put just a little shadow on him.

Perhaps one trouble with Thomas was that he had no important backing. He came from Virginia, and his state had seceded; he stayed with the Union, but when the war began, his state had no important representatives in Washington to push his cause. His merits spoke for themselves, but nobody else bothered to speak for them; at one point, when his name was up for promotion, Lincoln is supposed to have remarked, "Let the Virginian wait."

Thomas waited, and what he waited for never quite came . . . until long after his death, which may have been a little too late. Anyway, he is now the subject of a genuinely first-rate study in Francis F. McKinney's

Education in Violence, a book which is unreservedly recommended to anyone who wants to know more about one of the nation's greatest soldiers.

It appears from this, and from all the rest of the record, that Thomas got his reputation on the wrong basis. He was supposed to be the immovable man, the soldier who was indomitable and who stolidly dug in his heels and refused to be moved, and at places like Chickamauga he earned that reputation beyond question. When Rosecrans was driven back to Chattanooga, it was Thomas who stayed, formed a new line out of broken remnants of beaten men, held the line in spite of everything, and reduced the battle from an overwhelming disaster to a mere setback. Yet he was not primarily a defensive fighter. On the contrary he was aggressive and mobile, and he struck some of the most devastating offensive blows in all the war; and the legend that portrays him simply as a man who could hold the line when things went badly is a pronounced bit of miscasting.

It was Thomas who first cracked the Confederate line in Kentucky, unhinging its right wing in the Battle of Mill Springs early in 1862. It was Thomas who provided the essential stiffening for the Army of the Cumberland at Stones River and at Chickamauga; it was Thomas who managed to combine a care for details—provision of proper training, adequate uniforming and equipping, due attention to logistics—with the capacity for swift movement once the details had been taken care of. Twice in all the war a Federal army was able to look upon a Confederate army driven from the field in complete rout after a shattering Federal offensive; each time—at Chattanooga, and at Nashville—the fortunate and victorious army was commanded by Thomas.

Thomas shared one thing with Rosecrans: he was never quite able to hit it off with General Grant. In Rosecrans' case the trouble is fairly easy to see, but

---

Education in Violence: The Life of George H. Thomas and the History of the Army of the Cumberland, by Francis F. McKinney. Wayne State University Press. 530 pp. $9.50.

---

with Thomas it is more obscure. Somehow the two men just did not see eye to eye. Grant obviously respected Thomas' ability more than he respected Rosecrans', but the end result was about the same: when he became general in chief, Grant never had the confidence in Thomas which he had in men like Sherman, McPherson, and Sheridan, and as a result Thomas missed the full measure of credit which he had earned.

So Thomas' case is not quite like that of Rosecrans. Rosecrans did well but had one bad day which tarnished his fame. Thomas never had a bad day. With Rosecrans, one has the feeling: This man could have been the best of them all, except for that one mishap. With Thomas, one gets the haunting feeling: Perhaps this man actually was the best of them all, but it took his country the better part of a century to realize it.

Thomas was perhaps the one top-ranking Federal officer who knew just what to do with his cavalry. Even Sheridan did not come up to him there. Thomas, incidentally, was a trained cavalryman himself, and he saw cavalry in much the same ultramodern, nontraditional way as Confederate Bedford Forrest saw it—as a striking force which used horses simply because the horses gave men greater mobility but which did its fighting on foot. In the final months of the war Thomas put together (at the cost of an unending struggle with the War Department) a cavalry corps under young James H. Wilson which carried repeating rifles and could move through the South irresistibly, a force wholly outside of the tradition of Jeb Stuart and John Hunt Morgan: mechanized infantry, in substance, able to move faster than anyone else and also able to hit harder, one which ignored "brilliant" raids and struck at the enemy's main forces with devastating power.

All of this, perhaps, is matter for the student of military history. But Thomas gets out of military history, simply because he was a good deal more than merely a military technician. He was one of the gifted few who understood what the war was about, understood what the North had to do to win it, and went ahead and put his ideas into practice. And it was quite a while before this fact was generally recognized.

Perhaps Chickamauga did part of the damage. At Chickamauga Thomas fought as good a defensive battle as any man ever fought, and he was "the Rock of Chickamauga" forever after, immovable, imperturbable, and indomitable. Grant is supposed to have remarked once that Thomas was "too slow to move and too brave to run away." If Grant said that, he was wrong. There was nothing slow about Thomas. He liked to make sure that everything was ready before he moved, but when he did move, somebody had to get out of the way.

Mr. McKinney has written a very good book indeed, and it is essential reading for anyone who wants a full understanding of the human instruments with which the Federal government fought and won the Civil War. Thomas was one of the best of the lot. Yet he does remain a man who did not, in his lifetime at least, quite reach the summit of popular approval. Perhaps this is one case where the general verdict of history needs to be upgraded.

The Other Hill

Back to Chickamauga again: this time to take a look at the Confederate side. One of the gifted soldiers there was a withdrawn, somewhat cantankerous man named Daniel Harvey Hill, who commanded an army corps under Braxton Bragg and who, like most of Bragg's other top commanders, emerged from the battle feeling that the Confederacy had missed a great opportunity because of the failings of the man at the top.

Hill was "one of the two Hills" in Confederate memory. He and the Virginian A. P. Hill wrote their names large, on the record of the Army of Northern Virginia and in hot battle action. Perhaps A. P. Hill was the more fortunate: he died in action just before the war ended and was enshrined in the special legend that attached itself to the generals of the lost cause who did not outlive the cause itself. D. H. Hill survived the war by nearly a quarter of a century, and during all of the postwar years he spoke his mind vigorously. Since he had pronounced opinions about the merit of things done by himself and by others, and since he was frank beyond the bounds of prudence, he pulled controversy about himself like a blanket. Lee himself took a distaste to him, while the war was on and afterward, and this undoubtedly hurt Hill more than Grant's dislike hurt Rosecrans and Thomas. Hill has come down in memory as a capable soldier who just did not quite fit in anywhere.

He too needs another look, and a perceptive study of him is available in Hal Bridges' *Lee's Maverick General*. Reading this book, one is likely to feel that the Confederacy never really made the best use of this man's capacities. He was undeniably very difficult, in a way Rosecrans and Thomas were not, which is to say that he had a thorny personality and spoke his acidulous mind at times when he should have kept quiet. All the same, it is hard to escape the feeling that as a soldier he was an extremely good man to have on one's side. Not a man, probably, for the top command anywhere, but an extremely good subordinate for anyone who knew just how to use him.

Hill was frail, racked all his life by poor health, dyspeptic, morose, contentious. He won his reputation in the Army of Northern Virginia, and even in that army, whose untrained soldiers insisted that their generals must show an instinctive contempt for personal peril, he was famous as a man who did not know what fear was. He fought well whenever there was fighting to be done, but he argued about it afterward; he finally tried the patience of Lee beyond Lee's endurance, and after 1862 Lee concluded that the Con-

federacy would be just as well served if Hill did the rest of his fighting in someone else's army. Thereafter the man was on the perimeter.

He was rescued from obscurity late in 1863 when Jefferson Davis correctly concluded that Bragg needed more competent assistants. Hill became, temporarily, a lieutenant general, and went west to command one of Bragg's army corps. After the Battle of Chickamauga Bragg accused practically all of his subordinates of errors of one kind or another, and Hill was one of the ones he named; but from the record it appears that Hill, like the rest, did about as well as anyone could have done under the erratic leadership which was on display at general headquarters, and it is at least clear that Hill, when the battle ended, realized something which Bragg was unable to see—that the

---

Lee's Maverick General, Daniel Harvey Hill, by Hal Bridges. McGraw-Hill Book Co. 323 pp. $7.50.

Confederacy had won a great victory which might have important consequences if it could be followed up. Bragg simply sat and thought about it.

Along with others, Hill made outcry. The oddest feature of the Confederate victory at Chickamauga was the fact that a round dozen of Bragg's generals presently sent a letter to Jefferson Davis complaining that "complete paralysis" had fallen upon the victorious army and urging that Bragg be relieved of his command. Davis, unaccountably, refused to take action; and not long afterward, Hill ceased to be a lieutenant general and ceased to command troops in action. Except for minor assignments in the final days, Hill was finished.

All of that is understandable. Hill was too outspoken, too critical of others, too ready to remind his fellows of their faults; it takes a rare army to keep such a man in high command and make full use of him. Yet the man was a good soldier, and it is hard to quarrel very much with Mr. Bridges' summary—"a versatile and talented individualist, whose fighting career, marked by great achievement as well as great controversy, strongly suggests, when seen in full, that Harvey Hill was one of the ablest of Lee's lieutenants."

He was another man who did not quite make it. He missed making it, probably, by a wider margin than Rosecrans, certainly by a wider margin than Thomas. But he might have been placed higher than he was placed; he could have been used to better effect than the Richmond government did use him. And he compels a backward glance. He was alive, talented . . . and interesting.

This fanciful presentation of the Emancipation Proclamation, painstakingly bringing out the face of that document's author, is a fine example of 19th century steel or quill pen work. It comes from the Frederick Hill Meserve Collection in New York.